Architects of Power

So Charles
with my thanks
and best wishes

2010
at sea

Architects of Power

Roosevelt, Eisenhower,
and the American Century

PHILIP TERZIAN

BRIEF ENCOUNTERS

Encounter Books · New York · London

Copyright © 2010 by Philip Terzian

First American edition published in 2010 by Encounter Books, an activity of Encounter for Culture and Education, Inc., a nonprofit, tax exempt corporation.
Encounter Books website address: *www.encounterbooks.com*

Manufactured in the United States and printed on acid-free paper. The paper used in this publication meets the minimum requirements of ANSI/NISO Z39.48–1992 (R 1997) (*Permanence of Paper*).

FIRST AMERICAN EDITION

LIBRARY OF CONGRESS CATALOGING-IN-PUBLICATION DATA

Terzian, Philip.
Architects of power : Roosevelt, Eisenhower, and the American century / by Philip Terzian.
p. cm. — (Encounter broadsides)
Includes bibliographical references and index.
ISBN-13: 978-1-59403-378-0 (hardcover : alk. paper)
ISBN-10: 1-59403-378-1 (hardcover : alk. paper)
1. Roosevelt, Franklin D. (Franklin Delano), 1882–1945.
2. Eisenhower, Dwight D. (Dwight David), 1890–1969. 3. Roosevelt, Franklin D. (Franklin Delano), 1882–1945—Political and social views.
4. Roosevelt, Franklin D. (Franklin Delano), 1882–1945—Influence.
5. Eisenhower, Dwight D. (Dwight David), 1890–1969—Political and social views. 6. Eisenhower, Dwight D. (Dwight David), 1890–1969—Influence. 7. United States—Foreign relations—20th century.
8. Political leadership—United States—Case studies. 9. Great powers—Case studies. 10. Presidents—United States—Biography. I. Title.
E807.T39 2010
327.73009'04—dc22
2009038325

10 9 8 7 6 5 4 3 2 1

Contents

*To Grace, Hillman, Gracie
and the Hounds*

Apology

AS I WRITE, Congress is contemplating a memorial in Washington to Dwight D. Eisenhower, and the prospects are not encouraging. The press is almost uniformly hostile to the project, and ours is not an age of monuments—or not, at any rate, monuments of the sort Eisenhower would deserve. There has been a protracted debate among interested parties about its nature—between supporters of a "living memorial" and advocates for some kind of physical commemoration—and the proponents of a physical memorial seem to have prevailed. A site has been selected near the Air and Space Museum, adjacent to the Mall, and an architect has been chosen; but what kind of monument, exactly, would be built, or even whether anything will ultimately be constructed, remains unclear. Those who hold this slim volume in their hands, at the dawn of the second decade of the twenty-first century, will have a better idea how the episode played out; the author is left, in the meantime, to speculate.

The purpose of this essay is twofold. First, I want to set down some general propositions about the two public figures in the twentieth century who personify, in their lives, careers, and public philosophies, the rise of the United States of America to global leadership: Franklin D. Roosevelt and Dwight D. Eisenhower. I use the well-worn term "global leadership" advisedly. It may be argued that the world has witnessed, in our time, something like an American imperium; but it is an empire by default, not design. On the face of it, this is a primary difference between American suzerainty and the colonial aspirations of the classical era; of Carolingian France, Spain, and Great Britain; or even of comparatively smaller players such as Portugal or Wilhelmine Germany. Once the American republic realized its manifest destiny—involving, as it did, the conquest of native peoples and the forcible expulsion of the waning Spanish empire—the impulse to expansion was vanquished. America's role in the world has been a function of its maturity as an economic and industrial power, not the other way around. Even those furtive gestures in the direction of what we might call empire—the Monroe Doctrine at the beginning of the nineteenth century, the defeat of the Spanish empire in the Caribbean and western Pacific at the end of the nineteenth century, the purchase of Alaska in the middle of the nineteenth century—may be seen as prudential, defensive, and self-protective in spirit. Circumstances have conscripted American power in the world.

It is incorrect to suggest that the United States is a pre - ternaturally inward-looking nation, or that isolationism is the natural disposition of its citizens. America is, to some degree, historically isolated by geography, but that scarcely obtains in the modern world; and Americans have been engaged with the world, on an equal basis, by way of trade and manufacturing since before independence. (It might be said, in fact, that the colonies' economic self-sufficiency was a significant impulse toward political independence from Britain.) The real question is not whether Americans are prone to isolation or engagement, but how their engagement with the world has evolved, how events have con- spired to transport the United States toward world power, and how these developments have been guided by political leadership. For the great debates on foreign affairs in Amer- ican history have not been about whether to have debates on foreign affairs; they have been between and among com- peting visions of American influence in the world. The congressional isolationists of the 1930s were not devoid of vision about the uses of American power in Europe; the proponents and opponents in the League of Nations fight in 1919 did not pretend that the United States could choose to turn its back on the world. They differed in degree, not kind. The isolationists were resigned to the course of events in Europe; the interventionists sought to influence that course of events. Both understood that the United States enjoyed the capacity to exert power, but they differed on the means by which that power should be exercised. Among nations, the decision *not* to act is as pertinent—as potentially destruc- tive or salutary—as the decision to intervene.

This leads to a second purpose, which is a brief explo- ration of the uses to which historical memory may be put. I have mentioned the proposed memorial to Eisenhower. Not far from that site, at the opposite end of the Mall, a memorial to Franklin Roosevelt, conceived and dedicated a half-century after his death, does exist. As with any such public monument, it is a product of its times—which, it should be emphasized, were not the times in which Roosevelt lived and prospered. The Roosevelt memorial tells us con- siderably more about the 1990s than about the 1930s and 1940s, and in Roosevelt's case, this is both significant and unfortunate. It is significant because it allows us to see the extent to which posterity bends and shapes history to suit its needs; it is unfortunate because it has distorted Roosevelt's history to such an extent that recovery is an archaeological process, and the invocation of Roosevelt in our time can be misleading and illusory. To be sure, federal monuments scarcely constitute the historical record, and what the public knows about FDR and his presidency derives from scholarship and a written, sometimes visual, record, not from statuary. But in this instance, at least, the memorial embodies Roosevelt's modern reputation, which is very different from what he intended or accomplished in his lifetime.

Historical reputations rise and fall (and rise and fall again) with time, and the contemporary perspective on the past is never settled. But American policy is never generated in a vacuum, and the rationale for action is invariably grounded in experience. The nature of experience—its particular details, its lessons for the present—is at its heart a debate about policy, and is frequently decisive. But of course, if the past is viewed through a distorted lens—in effect, if we look closely at the Roosevelt memorial—then the future is ill-served by contemporary politics, which pursues short-term gain and not long-term objectives. Without a clear vision of the past, our knowledge of the present and perspective on the future may be dangerously myopic. If we cannot see the stricken world that Roosevelt inhabited and Eisenhower understood, we are less likely to see the perils (and challenges) of the world we have inherited.

This is not an idle speculation. The culture that seems natural to modern man, the culture we inhabit, was not always as it appears to be now, and the world is full of people and doctrines and historical trends that are not only hostile to the West and to the Western tradition in culture and politics, but aggressively hostile. The cost of democratic success and capitalist prosperity can be a kind of comfort, a sense of historical insouciance, that can also be a dangerous complacency. Roosevelt saw this, and Eisenhower understood it, and both acted upon their perceptions: in that sense, they were genuine servants of their people. The question for our time is whether we recognize this as well.

1 | The Hyde Park Roosevelt

In the dim distant past [my ancestors] may have been
Jews or Catholics or Protestants – What I am more
interested in is whether they were good citizens and
believers in God – I hope they were both.
                                    Franklin D. Roosevelt, 1935

THE GREAT American presidents are submerged in mythology, and Franklin Roosevelt is no exception. In understanding his character and seeking to assess his tenure in
the White House, his experience with infantile paralysis is
often considered paramount. According to this version,
prior to the onset of polio at the age of thirty-nine, FDR was
a feckless, attenuated youth, a frivolous socialite who
skimmed across the surface of life, content with a gentleman's C at Harvard and happy to accept the preferments
that seemed to come effortlessly his way. After he contracted
polio, Roosevelt came to understand disappointment, dis-
covered new depths of meaning in his life, and developed a
consuming empathy for those less fortunate than he. Suffering and physical impairment were the central emotional
events of his life, dividing his past self from the mature man
who rescued his country from the Depression and led
America during the Second World War.

That is the mythology—and like most myths, it is
grounded in a handful of facts deployed to concoct a particular narrative. In Roosevelt's case it is especially distorted
and misleading. Roosevelt was not a notably reflective man,

and what self-analysis he may have undertaken in his life-time he kept to himself; but he would have laughed at the notion that polio was anything other than an arbitrary dis-aster that afflicted him and tested, but did not shape, the man that he was. In most respects, FDR was the same person after 1921 than he had been before, and the elusive character and "deeply forested interior" had taken shape long before he became paraplegic. It is to Roosevelt's credit that his crip-pling disease did not scuttle his ambition but only diverted him from the path that he had undertaken in his youth. Polio, it may be assumed, hardened and disciplined his will, but it was a greater physical than emotional impediment. The astonishing fact that Roosevelt never discussed the implications of his affliction with anyone—including mem-bers of his own family—and never revealed the emotional toll of polio in any straightforward sense only conveys the depth of his ambition and reserve. The pursuit of the presidency, we may be assured, requires such personal resources, which FDR enjoyed in abundance.

He was, in fact, a familiar figure in American political history: a product of the upper-middle or upper classes for whom politics was a social inheritance and a natural incli-nation. In his centennial-year study of FDR, the journalist Joseph Alsop went to considerable lengths to explain that Roosevelt was *not* an aristocrat in the usual sense of the term, since the United States harbors no such social distinctions; but this merely serves to reveal the aristocrat that Roosevelt manifestly was. If, like a democratic American, he chose to explain himself in other ways, and went to some lengths to deplore such implications—in the manner of Alsop, for instance—he succeeded only in demonstrating the extent to which he was, by any measure, aristocratic in upbringing, manner, and outlook. Of course, "aristocracy" in this sense has less to do with superficial qualities than with natural presumptions, codes of conduct, and habits of being. Roosevelt was ostentatiously aware of his family background and of his relative status in the landed gentry of the Hudson River Valley and the early American republic. His immediate forebears were not only moneyed and prominent in civic, commercial, and social life but imitated the lives of the English rural gentry. His father James was a self-conscious and self-described country gentleman, the master of a minor estate who divided his existence between genteel business ventures and rural pursuits as well as the solemn duties of the local squirearchy. Like the Henry James inventions they resemble, the Roosevelts even migrated to Europe in season and participated in the New York–Boston matrimonial sweepstakes. Members of the Reformed church from their days in the Dutch ascendancy of seventeenth-century New York, they had become Episcopalians by the middle of the nineteenth century. Sufficiently conscious of their aboriginal status to avoid *nouveau riche* Newport, they migrated in the summertime to an island off the coast of Canada, safe from the contagion of post–Civil War wealth. When a Vanderbilt constructed an enormous mansion adjacent to the Roosevelt place, James Roosevelt refused their invitation to dine: malice disguised as gentility.

Yet there may be found in James Roosevelt's Victorian *hauteur* an element of uncertainty as well. He was, despite appearances, prone to gambling on the occasional business venture, as he sought to increase the family endowment. He also commended his older son James, Jr.—who, in contrast to his half-brother Franklin, really *was* feckless by nature—to appointive political and diplomatic offices, with mixed results but for reasons we can easily guess. And while Franklin was tutored at home until a certain age, James Roosevelt ultimately sent him to Groton—a new school founded outside Boston by the Reverend Endicott Peabody, an American-born (but Cambridge-educated) Episcopal clergyman—that was expressly devoted to the cultivation of a ruling class. We may disagree about the qualities and defects of such institutions, or the very existence of a governing class in a democratic society; but the fact is that James Roosevelt took these notions seriously and imparted them to his younger, and ultimately more consequential, son. It is also clear that the Peabody ethos took root in Franklin Roosevelt.

We know this for two reasons. First, there is the evidence that Roosevelt was not a success at Groton in the sense by which such qualities are measured in schoolboy terms. He was too slight to succeed as an athlete—his cousin Alice Roosevelt Longworth always derided the Hyde Park Roosevelt preference for sailing in contrast to the Oyster Bay Roosevelt habit of rowing—and, partly due to his solitary upbringing and delayed arrival at Groton, did not get on so well with his fellow students. He was hardly a pariah—not in the sense that his first cousin James Roosevelt, who seems to have been mentally disturbed, was a social outcast—but he was preternaturally accustomed to the company of older people and, in the words of one alumnus (the son of an FDR classmate), was altogether "too eager to please" his young contemporaries who, then as now, put a certain value on reserve. The qualities that served Roosevelt the politician well were not designed to endear him to late Victorian adolescent specimens of his class. By contrast, Roosevelt was an academic success, a better-than-average student who substituted managing the baseball team for playing and who wrote letters home full of artificial cheer and enthusiasm for his school. Roosevelt was an eager supplicant to the headmaster and his wife, who trained the boys in the Anglican faith; and no matter what his private feelings may have been about Endicott Peabody, Roosevelt never failed to pay public fealty to his old schoolmaster, enlisting him for service at his wedding ceremony and savoring the pleasure of summoning Peabody three times to officiate at his presidential inaugurations.

The second reason for crediting Peabody's influence on Roosevelt's life is somewhat less obvious. We may assume that Roosevelt took Peabody's admonitions about public service to heart because he entered politics (becoming the first—and thus far, the only—Groton alumnus to be elected president). But it is difficult to discern what, exactly, impelled Roosevelt to enter politics, especially since he was constitutionally indisposed to explain himself in such ways. One theory, which seems the least likely, is that his unhappiness at Groton—accentuated by his later failure to be elected to the exclusive Porcellian Club at Harvard—impelled him to take gradual vengeance on his classmates: first, by bucking the tide as a Democrat, and second, by surpassing their achievements in business or the law by serving as chief magistrate of the United States. This theory would make more sense if we did not know that James Roosevelt was already a Democrat, and that FDR was not the sort of youth to defy his father's direction in such matters. Moreover, Roosevelt seems to have settled on politics very early in his career as a lawyer in

New York—seems, indeed, to have mapped out a route to the White House, as described to a fellow junior member in the firm of Carter, Ledyard, and Milburn, that bore a striking resemblance to the path of his distant cousin, Theodore. It is true that elective politics was an unusual career choice for one of his time and station, and that the great majority of his contemporaries at Groton and Harvard and other citadels of the Protestant ascendancy were far more likely to enter business or finance or even one of the professions, or perhaps the church; but Roosevelt never felt obliged to enlarge what was, by any measure, a comfortable family fortune, and he was manifestly bored by the law. So Peabody's call to public service, combined with the example of his presidential cousin, led inexorably to politics.

The example of Theodore Roosevelt cannot be understated in Franklin Roosevelt's biography. The famous rivalry between the two branches of the family was a fact in FDR's adulthood: Franklin was a Democrat in a predominantly Republican clan; he was an active rival of Theodore's eldest son for supremacy in New York politics; and several Oyster Bay cousins were publicly derisive, even hostile, in their treatment of their Hyde Park relation after he entered the White House. Yet it is easy to ascribe too much to these facts and to ignore the tribal rites of the class to which both branches of the family belonged. That is to say, political differences did not necessarily translate into personal hostility, and in the Roosevelt family, at least, blood usually transcended political ideology. Even Theodore's elder daughter Alice Roosevelt Longworth, whose fame in later life was largely sustained by well-publicized remarks at her cousin's expense, was a frequent guest at the White House in Roosevelt's second term, and FDR remained on friendly, not to say affectionate, terms with innumerable streams from the main branch of the Oyster Bay Roosevelts—not least through his marriage to Theodore's niece. In this, as in most aspects of FDR's life, we may discern a dual impetus: he was certainly compelled by his upbringing to be conciliatory, even magisterial. But it must have given him pleasure to remind his cousins of his political triumphs, sometimes at their expense, and he surely reveled in his status as the sun around which the other Roosevelts revolved.

This impulse derived from the senior member of his family in national life. Theodore Roosevelt, declared his fifth cousin, was "the greatest man I ever knew," and for once we may be certain that FDR spoke with absolute sincerity: Roosevelt was not a hero-worshiper by instinct and tended to be jealous of contemporaries. But it is not difficult to imagine the effect that the hero of San Juan Hill and the boy-governor of New York must have had on his distant, impressionable cousin when Theodore Roosevelt visited Groton to talk to the boys. Franklin was beginning his sophomore year at Harvard when Theodore became president—by accident, to be sure, but at the early age of 42 and, at the juncture of the twentieth century, seemingly by historical design. Whatever qualities Franklin discerned in his cousin Eleanor—the daughter of Theodore's late, unlamented brother Elliott, and a late-blooming swan—her connection to her uncle the president must have been paramount in FDR's mind. Roosevelt was doubtless attracted to the young Eleanor for her own sake, and it is certainly plausible that these two lonely products of privilege found some emotional refuge in each other; but the Roosevelt were dynasts as much as democrats, and

Eleanor's status must surely have separated her from the other young women of a certain station in New York. Roosevelt was already calculating his acquisition of power, made all the more precise by his seeming casualness and lack of ambition, and this was a shrewd marriage that would immediately usher him into the White House. Eleanor was given away by her uncle at their wedding; there was a famous scene at the reception where the president's dynamic presence drew the company away, leaving the newlyweds abandoned in an adjacent room. Abandoned, perhaps, but from the groom's point of view happily so, considering the dividends.

2 | President-in-Waiting

GRENVILLE CLARK, who shared quarters with FDR when they were both apprentice lawyers in Manhattan, testified that Roosevelt once explained to him the trajectory of his political ambitions: he intended to be elected to the New York state legislature, then secure an appointment as assistant secretary of the Navy and serve as governor of New York before attempting the presidency.

This is a remarkable anecdote, for two reasons. First, it reveals an overweening ambition in Roosevelt at a time in his life when no one, including members of his family, discerned anything remotely resembling professional, much less political, ambition in the amiable young man his cousins called "the Feather Duster." Second, FDR's plan is an exact parallel to Theodore's curriculum vitae, down to the Harvard degree. Assuming that Roosevelt actually said such a thing—and Clark, a public-spirited pillar of the Bar later in life, was not the inventive sort—it also reveals a particular clairvoyance. In 1907 or thereabouts Roosevelt might well have contemplated a candidacy for the New York state legislature in the near future—he was, in fact, elected to the state Senate three years later—but he could hardly have known, especially in that political epoch, that a Democratic administration would have put a sub-Cabinet post within his reach so soon. Yet if Roosevelt was thinking in dynastic terms, it was not an unreasonable notion: Theodore had been 39 years old when he was appointed assistant secretary of the Navy in the McKinley administration; Franklin might well have calculated that a similar opportunity would afford itself when he reached the same age, in 1921.

As we know now, the chronology was accelerated: FDR was appointed assistant secretary of the Navy at the age of 31, and except for a feint at a U.S. Senate seat two years later, he kept a length or two ahead of Theodore Roosevelt during the following decade. Theodore had been McKinley's running mate at the age of 41, but FDR was the Democratic vice-presidential candidate at 38, the same age Theodore was when he had been appointed assistant secretary of the Navy. Thereafter, as we also know, disaster intervened: Roosevelt was struck down by infantile paralysis the following year, and his political future—indeed, the course of his life—became suddenly and unexpectedly ambiguous.

Because FDR was, ultimately, only momentarily deflected from his object, despite his paraplegic status and uncertain health, we know that the one ingredient that motivated Franklin Roosevelt—ambition—was wedded to the particular trait he shared with Theodore Roosevelt—confidence. We may even say that FDR's ambition, in political terms at least, exceeded his distant cousin's. FDR was aware that the device that had propelled Theodore ahead of his class was his resignation from the Navy Department in 1898 and his organization of an irregular cavalry regiment in the war against Spain. After San Juan Hill, it is impossible to speculate where politics might have led Theodore Roosevelt had he been content to remain in political office. But no such opportunity presented itself to FDR: although Theodore persistently admonished his niece's husband to resign from the Navy Department after the United States entered the war against Germany, Franklin could not resist the entreaties of the Secretary of the Navy, Josephus Daniels, to remain in place, nor did he choose to appeal Woodrow Wilson's re - fusal to allow senior federal officials to enter military service. Either his sense of obligation to his political master, in his time, was greater than Theodore Roosevelt's in his, or Franklin's primary loyalty was to his political ambition.

Whereas Theodore felt obliged, both to himself and to his sense of public duty, to serve in the Army, Franklin Roosevelt could never quite conceive the circumstances that would propel him into the uniformed Navy. A cynical observer might assume that, while Theodore's service was conspicuous in the war against Spain, FDR was in no position to lead a well-publicized cavalry charge or otherwise attract public attention. In any event, it made no difference. Roosevelt remained assistant secretary and made the most of his fortunate circumstances; and within two months of the end of the First World War, Theodore Roosevelt was dead and his distant cousin's famous surname no longer stood in the way of Franklin's nomination as the 1920 Democratic vice-presidential candidate. Roosevelt knew that the 1920 campaign would be an exercise in futility—fought, as it was, on the dead issue of the League of Nations and freighted, as it was also, by Wilson's unpopularity—but it was a personal opportunity. He was transformed from a secondary figure in the Wilson administration into a national political figure, and no one was likely to blame him for the outcome of a race between Governor Cox and Senator Harding, both of Ohio.

Polio might or might not have decisively affected

Roosevelt's character—I believe it did not—but it inarguably complicated his political schedule. Of course, he could hardly have anticipated this; nor could he have conceived that what appeared to be a catastrophe—paralysis, withdrawal from active political life, a prolonged struggle to gain some measure of personal equilibrium—would be, in the long run, to his advantage. But this outcome was less about good fortune than it was a testament to the combination of ambition and confidence in Roosevelt's makeup. At a time when the members of his family were inclined to see him retire from public life and take up his father's mantle as local squire—collecting his books, stamps, and naval prints, refurbishing the Roosevelt place at Hyde Park, assuming the mantle of civic dignitary—Roosevelt seems never to have lost sight of his objective. It is generally understood that his mother and wife battled over Roosevelt's prospects, and that Eleanor prevailed when Franklin was persuaded *not* to retreat to Hyde Park. That is the public version of events, and there may be an element of truth in it. But it's more likely that the struggle between Sara and Eleanor Roosevelt was only incidentally about Franklin: it is far more plausible that Eleanor, who had long resented her domineering mother-in-law, did not wish to fall inexorably into the Hyde Park orbit, and that promoting Franklin's political career was a suitable device to prevent this. Whether this was motivated by disdain for Sara Roosevelt, faith in FDR's prospects for advancement, or resentment at her husband's recent infidelity, we cannot say: the Roosevelts did not live in an age when such matters were discussed in the open, especially not in that particular family. But the upshot is that, for both personal and professional reasons, Roosevelt's ambition prevailed—even if, in medical terms, it taxed his diminished resources and shortened his life.

What was the source of this ambition? We can never know, because FDR, despite his lifelong habit of correspondence and love of talk, was an especially self-protective, even secretive man whose interior life was entirely concealed from others, including—perhaps especially—his closest relations. The devices by which he compensated for this are all too evident: like most men possessed by presidential ambition, Roosevelt had hundreds of acquaintances but no close friends. He wrote thousands of letters that are little more than cheerful, sometimes anodyne, chatter, and his love for the spoken word chiefly manifested itself in domestic monologues, banter, and political rhetoric.

Roosevelt, like most politicians in a mass democracy, must remain an enigma to those who would comprehend him. His peculiar character might have been the consequence of his singular upbringing, spent as it was in a vast, highly privileged estate as the only child of an elderly father and a suffocating mother. Or it might have been sharpened by the shock of his arrival at Groton—more spartan, more intrusive, more bewildering than anything he had known in his brief experience—or, perhaps, by his notorious failure to be elected to the Porcellian Club at Harvard, the kind of disappointment that is especially devastating to adolescents. But we cannot know the answer to these questions. Other men have endured similar circumstances, suffered similar reverses, with different consequences. Roosevelt himself never furnished a hint about his motivation, and those who postulate such connections usually have some hypothesis to prove.

The only axiom we can confidently assert is that Roose - velt's decision to subsume his personal life to public ambi- tion was arrived at early, was profound, and was wedded to that innate confidence that was the hallmark of his cousin and, strictly speaking, most successful politicians. It mani- fested itself in his tenure in the New York Senate, where he repeatedly and at times obtusely defied his party, and it cer- tainly could be seen in his tenure at the Navy Department, where his impatience for advancement and relentless insubordination toward his chief, toward lawful authority, and even toward the stated policies of the Wilson adminis- tration had to be repeatedly forgiven, often by the admiring and ever-indulgent secretary, Josephus Daniels.

The relationship between Daniels and Roosevelt was an interesting and revealing one. Daniels was a Southern edi- tor of relatively humble origins, a Baptist teetotaler and small-d democrat with an aversion to the pomp and hierar- chy of the uniformed Navy and inclinations toward the pacifism of his idol, Secretary of State William Jennings Bryan. Roosevelt, by contrast, was a progressive of his day with imperial ambitions for the United States who reveled in the exercise of power, political and military. It is poignant to read the contemptuous exchanges between Franklin and Eleanor Roosevelt and their friends about the bumptious Daniels, who seems never to have perceived his assistant secretary's attitude nor lost his obvious affection for this subordinate who was not of his choosing. In his way, FDR made amends as president: he gave Daniels a cherished diplomatic appointment, and Daniels' son Jonathan served on the White House press staff. (It was the younger Daniels who first publicly revealed the clandestine affair between

Roosevelt and Lucy Mercer, two decades after FDR's death.)

Cloaking all of this minor melodrama, however, was Roosevelt's familiar affect: his direct language to Daniels was always extravagantly deferential, and his correspondence, especially in later years, was purposefully cheerful, even bantering. As might be expected, when circumstances reversed their status, Roosevelt continued to call Daniels "Chief" and insisted that Daniels refrain from addressing him as "Mr. President"—very nearly the only person to whom FDR accorded that privilege. We may speculate why Daniels, of all FDR's political associates—and this would extend to such disparate figures as Louis Howe, Samuel Rosenman, Henry Morgenthau, Sumner Welles, Harry Hopkins, and others—was kept on familiar terms, but it could be said that while others were Roosevelt's natural allies or boon companions, Daniels was the one who served the president's purposes for FDR's sake, not his own. Roosevelt, in his indirect fashion, understand this, and responded in the way his upbringing had taught him to behave.

Wendell Willkie once asked Roosevelt why he kept Harry Hopkins, who was something of a political liability, so close —literally so, with Hopkins residing in the White House during the Second World War—to which FDR responded by saying that if Willkie were someday to be president, he too would value someone who sought nothing for himself except the opportunity to serve. Roosevelt might well have believed this, although he could hardly have been unaware of Hopkins' own agenda; but this tells us something about the chasm that separated FDR from ordinary human relationships, as well as the isolation of the presidency. That was the price of Roosevelt's ambition, which he willingly paid.

Nor did it fail him at a moment of opportunity. Roosevelt had kept himself active during his convalescence, and incurred a particular debt when he twice put in nomination for the presidency the name of Alfred E. Smith. He had been reluctant to run for governor of New York in 1928, as Smith wished him to do, fearing that Smith's cataclysmic loss to Herbert Hoover, which he anticipated, would drag him under and destroy his own prospects. But FDR would not have been himself if he could resist entreaties to take a chance at being governor—to return, in literal terms, to the track laid down by Theodore Roosevelt—and his particular skills enabled him to withstand Smith's loss and prevail in his own race.

In Albany Roosevelt not only established himself in the public mind as a capable executive—pursuing the sort of internal improvements that were the hallmark of progressivism in the 1920s—but after October 1929 and, especially, the midterm elections of 1930, was able to position himself to strike at the incumbent president. Whether Roosevelt's ambition could have been rewarded in the absence of a national emergency we cannot know; but the first duty of a politician is to get himself elected, and if that is achieved by way of misfortune, so be it.

3 | "War is a contagion"

IN 1956 T. S. ELIOT wrote a curious letter to an Episcopal priest in New York, a personal friend of Eliot's and admirer of FDR who had presented Eliot with a dinner plate that had once belonged to the Roosevelt family and been used at Hyde Park. With elaborate courtesy, Eliot asked to return the gift, "not because I impugn [Roosevelt's] character or his motives. . . . [But I] cannot forget . . . that Mr. Roosevelt was no great friend of England; that he was suspicious of British policy and disapproving of the existence of the (now almost nonexistent) British Empire."

His correspondent, so far as I know, did not choose to argue the point, especially since Eliot assured him that "I have long since ceased to take sides in American party politics." But it is worth noting that so acute an observer of modern culture as Eliot—whose attitude toward politics, if not party politics, was not nearly so disinterested as he implied—should have been so extravagantly mistaken about Roosevelt's foreign policy, not to say his attitude toward Great Britain. Roosevelt was, in the words of Winston Churchill, "the greatest American friend Britain has ever known," and while we may to some degree discount the lapidary words of admiring politicians, Churchill could easily have expressed himself in more guarded terms. To be sure, Churchill spoke those words when Britain was at its most importunate: in 1946 the relative positions of Britain and the United States in the world were newly fixed; and Churchill, although out of office, believed that paying fealty to the late president—who had, after all, been his comrade-in-arms during the war against Hitler—was in his country's interest. We know, of course, that Churchill's personal attitude largely coincided with his public pronouncements about FDR, and about the United States—even if we may speculate that Roosevelt did not always fully reciprocate those feelings. But this is to ignore a fundamental truth of history, and statecraft: that the first allegiance of every national leader is to his own country.

So let us proceed with this observation: that Franklin Roosevelt, upon assuming the presidency, did so in the midst of a national economic crisis and concentrated his energies on domestic affairs. But while this is true, and dominates histories of the period, it is only half the picture of the times; for Roosevelt was a player on the world stage from 1933 on. Nor was this an innovation at the time. Even if we recognize that American foreign policy during the 1920s reflected a deliberate choice to stand aside from what we would now call global commitments, it was hardly impervious to the world. Nor was it uninvolved. Just as Calvin Coolidge concentrated his energies on retiring the Allied debt from the Great War, his predecessor Warren Harding was preoccupied with disarmament—and was successful, in the context of the times. Moreover, the eminence that propelled Herbert Hoover to the presidency was grounded in his unprecedented efforts to relieve suffering in Europe before the American entry into the First World War. Indeed, if we may identify any one American as the author of the premise that the problems of the world demand American involvement, it would be Hoover. FDR's cousin Theodore had dabbled in diplomacy during the Russo-Japanese war, and had sought to project American power by way of the Panama Canal, the Great White Fleet, and a dozen other projects—not excluding his own personal diplomacy in Europe after leaving the White House. But it was Hoover during 1914–17 who established the precedent of American assistance to a distressed Europe; Woodrow Wilson's declaration of war against Germany, delayed as it was, was only the logical next step.

This is not the place to enumerate Hoover's presidential efforts to grapple with the economic slump in Europe, which was exacerbated by the Wall Street crash, or his close relations with those European statesmen—British, French, and German—who sought in the late 1920s and early 1930s to preserve the peace in an increasingly fractured Europe. The United States may have chosen to stand aside from the League of Nations, but it was Hoover's predecessor Coolidge who presided over the efforts to outlaw war—a gesture we now recognize as futile, even dangerously naïve, but only with the experience of hindsight.

This, then, was the diplomatic presidency that Roosevelt inherited: an ambiguous presence in the councils of the West and exile from Geneva, but also the growing recognition that the balance of power was moving relentlessly westward across the Atlantic. Indeed, Roosevelt's first gesture toward exercising American power was to participate in—and then indirectly scuttle—the economic conference that had been assembled in London to grapple with the collapse of the global banking system. This had a calamitous effect abroad, and led to some disarray within his own administration.

(The undersecretary of the Treasury, Dean Acheson, was obliged to resign, and his chief, secretary William Woodin (by then fatally ill), slowly withdrew from office, to be replaced in due course by Roosevelt's compliant financier-neighbor, Henry Morgenthau.) But Roosevelt was distracted not just by dire circumstances in the American economy but by ominous developments across the ocean. Whereas Coolidge and Hoover had dealt with a generation of well-intentioned politician-statesmen—Sir Austen Chamberlain, Ramsay Macdonald, Gustav Stresemann, Heinrich Brüning, Aristide Briand, Leon Blum—Roosevelt was confronted by fundamental changes in the character of the European governments. The Bolsheviks, having consolidated their power in the old Russian empire, were embarking on the Stalinist terror; Mussolini had invented a hybrid doctrine of uniformed nationalism in Italy that was gaining admirers in the United States; and barely five weeks before FDR's inauguration, Adolf Hitler became chancellor of Germany.

It is fair to say that Roosevelt, as a creature of his times, looked upon these developments with an element of equanimity. The Russian Revolution was not especially admired in the United States, but certain aspects of the Soviet state —in particular, its planned and centralized economy— appealed to certain academic theorists, especially those who had despaired of democratic capitalism. The Roosevelt administration sheltered some such harbingers of a totalitarian future. Roosevelt always looked upon Mussolini with an admixture of amusement and contempt—the dictator's theatrical style and bombastic rhetoric offended FDR's sense of decorum—but his concern about Il Duce was based more on Mussolini's appeal to his fellow Europeans than any threat constituted by Italy. This was not, of course, the case with Germany; and while it is fair to guess that certain aspects of Hitler's domestic program find some parallels in the New Deal—the mass recruitment of the young unemployed for public works, the use of artists and writers to exalt the newly energetic state, the use of propaganda and public spectacle to translate policies into public opinion—Roosevelt, unlike some democratic statesmen of the era, never suffered any illusions about Hitler's nature. Support for Hitler and the Nazi regime among Americans is habitually overstated: Hitler, like any foreign despot, had his American admirers, and in the 1930s the connection of some German-Americans to the land of their birth or recent ancestry was stronger than we can now appreciate. But from 1933 on Roosevelt recognized that the strength of Nazi Germany was achieved at the expense of European democracy, and that Hitler's intentions—his undisguised anti-Semitism, the sense of grievance about the Versailles settlement that he nursed, his steady aggrandizement of German arms and traditional German nationalist aspirations—were almost wholly malign.

And yet, Roosevelt also recognized that the European state of affairs put him in a dangerous quandary. Just as the European democracies, notably Britain and France, the guarantors of the 1918 status quo, were increasingly irresolute, so Hitler was correspondingly emboldened. But the United States was in no position to influence events, even indirectly. The neutrality acts that were deliberately intended to insulate America from involvement in European affairs were not only binding but politically popular. Moreover, while it is difficult to conceive in our day, the armed forces were then not just starved of patronage and resources but regarded in some quarters as a provocation to the outside world and a symbol of calamity. A famous poster-advertisement of the time depicted a veteran of the Great War in a wheelchair under the headline, "Hello, Sucker!"—echoing a famous phrase of the 1920s, unconnected to politics but reflecting a marked contempt and indifference toward those who bore arms in the nation's defense.

Roosevelt comprehended the gathering danger in these circumstances, and he was not the only one to do so. It is tempting, in retrospect, to suppose that FDR stood alone against the tide of isolationism that swept the United States during this inter-war period, but it is hardly accurate. The gray eminences who had guided the United States to world power in the wake of the Spanish-American War—William Howard Taft, Elihu Root, Charles Evans Hughes, Henry Stimson, Charles Dawes, and others—were still active in public affairs (Taft, indeed, was chief justice throughout the 1920s, and Hughes held the same position in the 1930s). And they were active on behalf not of partisan isolation but of increased American involvement in European affairs. Their advocacy took the form of institutions that were founded to advance American prospects for world leadership, such as the Council on Foreign Relations, or were designed, like the World Court, to move America along in harmony with the League of Nations. We know how impotent the League turned out to be, and the verdict on international jurisprudence is mixed; but these were symbolic matters as well as substantive ones, and advocates of American power had an ally in Roosevelt.

If there had ever been doubts about Roosevelt among

these early architects of American participation in world affairs, they were effectively answered when he traveled to Chicago in 1937 to speak at the dedication of a bridge. No doubt this choice was deliberate: the Middle West was the heartland of isolationism, and Chicago was its citadel, while civic improvement was a subject that transcended principled differences. Roosevelt did not speak with the intention of offending his immediate audience, and it may be argued that his audience was not only the Americans who comprehended his message but those Europeans—that is to say, Hitler and, to a lesser degree, Hitler's potential adversaries in any war—who might have speculated about the intentions of the world's pre-eminent industrial power. Most of the "Quarantine Speech" consists of the sort of inconsequential observations that could be made under almost any circumstances; but in turning from a generalized hope for peace to a specific posture, Roosevelt signaled that his intent as president was unchanged from his days as a student when he followed Theodore Roosevelt's lead in establishing the United States as first among global powers.

His point was simple and, on the face of it, obvious: the United States had long supported and promoted efforts toward the establishment of peace, and these had largely consisted of appeals to harmony and the codification of disarmament. The interests of the United States were fundamental: American prosperity required a global marketplace, and discord interfered with prosperity. Peace is good for business, in other words; but the pursuit of peace is more than just the conclusion of a multi-power treaty or a global pledge to outlaw war. If powers emerge in the world that threaten global peace, they implicitly threaten not only the national integrity of the United States but explicitly harm American prosperity. In the midst of the Depression, an appeal to prosperity might have seemed fanciful, at best; but Roosevelt was smart to marry America's mercantile destiny to its practical future as a world power. Nor did he fail to describe this in direct terms: "The will for peace on the part of peace-loving nations," he said, "must express itself to the end that nations that may be tempted to violate their agreements and the rights of others will desist from such a course."

"War is a contagion," he had declared earlier, "whether it is declared or undeclared . . . [and] we are determined to keep out of war. Yet we cannot insure ourselves against the disastrous effects of war and the dangers of involvement." And then, in the next sentence, is the substance of Roosevelt's dilemma: "We are adopting such measures as will minimize our risk of involvement"—in effect, a meaningless gesture in the direction of neutrality—"but we cannot have complete protection in a world of disorder in which confidence and security have broken down." Which is to say, it is well to wish for the best, and to work to ensure peace; but peace is not just the absence of conflict but also the conditions under which the interests of the United States are guaranteed, whether by global consent or by the exercise of power. Roosevelt preceded and followed these words with uncontroversial observations about the virtues of peace and the horrors of war, but his meaning was clear and suitably ambitious: he was prepared to transform the official neutrality of American policy, and he was equally prepared to enlist the United States in any challenge to Hitler's ambitions. The fact that he had neither the statutory authority nor the popular support to sustain these declarations is interesting, and Hitler (among others) was quick to recognize that the rhetoric of this particular address was unaccompanied by substance. But it was, by any measure, a transformative moment in American history, a deliberate and unambiguous break with the past and a challenge to convention, at home and abroad.

4 | "Doctor Win-the-War"

KENNETH S. LYNN, writing about FDR's deception of his wife in the Lucy Mercer affair, lamented that Roosevelt's most worshipful biographer, Arthur Schlesinger, Jr., failed to recognize the parallels between his private and public behavior. "An airy duplicity," he wrote, "a brazen hypocrisy, were hallmarks of the Rooseveltian presidency. Dangers at home and abroad may have necessitated such conduct, but the point is that FDR was an instinctive deceiver and always had been."

These are harsh words, but they are not untrue. Nor are they necessarily a judgment on Roosevelt's presidency. We know that, whatever the circumstances of his childhood and youth may have been, they instilled in Roosevelt a compulsive desire, an instinctive need, to conceal his genuine thoughts from everyone he knew or came in contact with— including, to some degree, himself, judging from his various diaries and journals. From very early in life he developed the dual talents of charm and artful deception, combined with an enigmatic manner and personality. One may suppose that these were psychic defenses or aberrations, but one may also argue that they are useful tools in a politician's arsenal. Roosevelt's compulsion to deceive was not necessarily malign; it could disguise a host of emotions and presumptions, which may have suited his purposes. His wife, writing obliquely about his marital deceptions, thought that utility governed his attitude toward those around him, including members of his family: he might have ranked his fellow human beings on the basis of their usefulness. But in Roosevelt's case this larger cause had historic consequences. His presidency was decisive in American history and, in due course, helped determine the course of World War II and the postwar order.

We have already seen the extent to which Roosevelt inherited the ambition of American progressives of an earlier generation to extend their franchise by exporting American power. This is not the place to argue about American exceptionalism—whether it is a rare gesture of national humility or a disguise for familiar national ambitions—but Roosevelt certainly believed that the status of the United States was unique among nations, including the world's democracies; and there is no evidence that he harbored reservations about American power and engagement in the world. In his youth he had been an enthusiastic supporter of the Spanish-American war, which catapulted his cousin to the White House; at Harvard he endorsed the (Theodore) Rooseveltian ambition for moral leadership in the world. His tenure in the Navy Department was marked by a long struggle against the restraints of his chief, who was suspicious of military power, and a persistent campaign to marry military strength to Woodrow Wilson's vision of a global order under American leadership. In his 1920 campaign for the vice presidency, he supported the League of Nations not because he exalted peace at the expense of American power but because he believed that the exercise of American power required American participation in global organizations.

He knew that American economic strength underwrote the potential for American power, and that the element missing in the politics of the 1920s was the will to direct such power to national ends. As we have seen, American policy in the postwar era was not "isolationist" in the strict sense of withdrawal from the councils of diplomacy—the United States eagerly participated in innumerable disarmament schemes —but Roosevelt believed that such gestures, as exercises in themselves, were meaningless: the Europeans were unlikely to abide by American guidelines, and Americans were unwilling to enforce their convictions.

This situation set the stage, by the end of Roosevelt's second term as president, for the most serious challenge to democracy in its history: the rise in Europe of left- and right-wing authoritarian powers, based in ideology and driven by traditional nationalist instincts. Roosevelt, by nature, was willing to adopt certain elements of fascist and communist rule—we may see this in his public works projects and his various efforts at civilian mobilization—but he had no instinctive attraction to right or left, only a generalized belief in "progress" and a firm conviction that the institutions of American democracy required reform, not revolution. Roosevelt had no illusions about the nature of the political systems or leadership in Soviet Russia, fascist Italy, Imperial Japan or Nazi Germany; but he did recognize that Russia's fundamentally defensive posture—the defense of its historic empire and access to the sea—stood in contrast to the unapologetically expansionist ambitions of Germany and, to a lesser degree, Italy. It is interesting to note that whereas Winston Churchill recognized in Hitler a new and significantly more sinister element in German history,

Roosevelt tended to think of German fascism in the terms of an earlier generation—with a declared horror at German militarism and Prussian autocracy, as if Hitler's designs were the logical extension of Bismarck's unification. Once again, this tells us more about the indelible effect of Roosevelt's youth on his thinking as an adult—his parents' annual pilgrimage to the spa at Bad Nauheim and their contempt for Teutonic manners—than about his understanding of political ideology, especially such perverse forms as fascism or National Socialism. It may also explain Roosevelt's attitude toward the urgent problem of the Jews in occupied Europe, believing as he must have done that German behavior in the Second World War would be, in all probability, indistinguishable from its behavior in the First. Nevertheless, for whatever reason, Roosevelt not only recognized the implicit danger that Germany posed to Europe (and, by extension, to the United States) in the 1930s, he eagerly assumed the mantle of democracy's chief advocate and defender at a moment, in the West, when such sentiments were distinctly unfashionable.

Thus, in Chicago in 1937, he not only sought to "quarantine" the dictatorships by mutual action of the Western democracies, but he proposed that the United States become the "arsenal of democracy" at a time when Europe was un - prepared to contemplate the conflict that Roosevelt believed inevitable. It is difficult, in retrospect, to appreciate the degree to which Roosevelt was not just prescient but brave, in his way. The intellectual consensus about democracy, on both sides of the Atlantic, was uncertain at best: there has been no other time, the 1960s included, in which belief in democracy was as delicate as it was in that decade. As the democratic leaders of Europe struggled with the twin burdens of economic stasis and diplomatic ferment, they had grown cynical, even despairing, about the principles at stake. Moreover, the Europeans approached Germany from a perspective that the United States did not, and could not, share: it was Europe that had been the battleground when the old order collapsed in 1914, taking with it a generation of young men and leaving in its wake an underlying suspicion that the development of mechanized weapons, in particular air power, made warfare not just obsolescent but futile. Stanley Baldwin, who lost two sons on the Western Front in the 1914–18 war, believed that "the bomber will always get through," and the vision of aerial warfare in the popular culture was not dissimilar to the fear of nuclear annihilation in the cold war era.

As his one-sided correspondence with the governments of Britain and France reveals, Roosevelt alone had faith in the notion of collective action to counteract Hitler and Mussolini. That is why he undertook to challenge Hitler publicly about his intentions, and why he sought to encourage Neville Chamberlain in his personal contacts with Hitler. Of course, Hitler famously derided FDR's approach, knowing as he did that Roosevelt was hampered by the neutrality laws, which seemed to have been designed specifically to tie Roosevelt's hands. And it is why Chamberlain, whose imagination was entirely backward-looking, failed to grasp the opportunity for collective resistance that Roosevelt offered. The British, not without reason, were uncertain about the depth of American commitment to Roosevelt's ambition, and in 1938–39 it was presumed that someone else would be president of the United States after 1940.

By the time Roosevelt had been elected to an unprecedented third term, the situation was not only different, but lethal. Hitler's re-militarization of the Rhineland was a fact, as were his garden invasions of Austria and Czechoslovakia. Britain and France had recognized that there was no longer any means of escape from conflict, but their capacity to act upon this knowledge was self-limited. It is here, of course, that we may recognize the importance of a single personality —namely Churchill—in reversing a self-destructive course; but we know that Churchill, for all his inspiring rhetoric and rear-guard actions on land and sea, recognized that American participation in the war against Hitler was not just desirable but imperative. That is why Churchill's secondary aim after June 1940 was to cultivate Roosevelt, even though he must have understood that the price of an American alliance against Hitler was the end of Britain's primacy as a world power. And it is for that reason, among others, that Roosevelt was a willing co-conspirator with Churchill, not only in confronting the Germans at sea and by furnishing assistance "short of war," but in circumventing the apparent will of the American people, reflected as it was in public opinion and congressional action.

Here, certainly, was the decisive moment when Roosevelt's favored method of operation—stealth and indirection, even deception, coupled with lofty pronouncements to the contrary—unhorsed the course of events in Europe and defined the postwar order. The period between Roosevelt's election in 1940 and the Japanese attack on Pearl Harbor has no parallel in American history. Despite every effort of Congress to enforce American neutrality, not to mention the gathering strength of popular isolationist movements such as the America First Committee, Roosevelt conducted his undeclared naval war against German shipping, sought to neutralize Japan by depriving its military leadership of the tools of warfare, and undertook an informal alliance with Britain by meeting with Churchill in neutral waters and offering a series of pronouncements, in the form of the Atlantic Charter, that served as a codification of American war aims four months before America entered the war.

In the midst of all this, and in characteristic fashion, Roosevelt repeated his assertion that American soldiers would not fight in foreign wars—unless, as he parenthetically stated, the United States was attacked—and he deliberately misled the public not only about his ulterior intentions but about the facts of America's naval engagements with Germany. His "assurance and reassurance" about the safety of American boys was confidently stated in the knowledge that Germany was not likely to attack the United States, especially after the invasion of Russia in June 1941; and his deceptions about the extent of American assistance to the British, and U.S. provocations of Germany at sea, only dramatize Hitler's relatively restrained response. Lend-Lease, which was intended to supply the British in rough compliance with American neutrality, was not so much a threat to Germany as a balm to England; the skirmishes in the North Atlantic, however, were both costly and dangerous, to both Germany and the United States.

The fact that this ambiguous state of affairs was resolved by Japan, and not Germany, is one of the minor ironies of World War II: Hitler chose to declare war on the United States in solidarity with his sometime ally, but Roosevelt had fully expected—had done very nearly all within his power—to see his orchestrated climax take place in the Atlantic, not the Pacific. Pearl Harbor, however, had two salutary effects: it reminded Americans that their country— the country that American nationalists had long conceived as stretching from coast to coast—looked toward the Pacific as well as the Atlantic; and it affirmed that the United States would not just pay a price for its willful disengagement but was vulnerable in ways that isolationism could not defend. Pearl Harbor did not just draw the United States into a wider scale of operations but exploded the notion that self-sufficiency and generous impulses were sufficient to defend America. This is a lesson that may have seemed obvious the morning after the attack, when FDR accepted the surrender of Congress and the war declaration was enacted; but it is a lesson that has been periodically forgotten, to our detriment.

Roosevelt, by his actions, maneuvered his country to meet the challenge of German and Japanese aggression, and he played a generous role in shaping the postwar world. But he did not eradicate the isolationist impulse in the American republic. There are two reasons for this. First, such sentiments are entrenched in the American character, as befits a nation largely settled by economic and political refugees; and second, it may be argued that Roosevelt's sleight-of-hand was tactically shrewd but strategically unsound. By talking about the virtues of passivity and affecting a determination to remain neutral in action as well as thought, all while preparing the political landscape for war, Roosevelt generated strong public sentiment to settle scores and win the conflict with Japan and Germany—but not necessarily a willingness to embrace the kind of global responsibility Roosevelt had in mind. Roosevelt understood the magnitude of American strength and potential, but he did not translate that understanding into public appreciation of the necessity for the exercise of American power in the world. In the course of the war he explained that his domestic agenda was to be suspended for the duration of the conflict, and that Americans who recognized "Doctor New Deal" were now in the service of "Doctor Win-the-War." This was the sort of homely device that FDR used to disguise his strategic purposes in political terms, and as always, it worked well. But it would not work indefinitely, as it implied that in due course Doctor Win-the-War would be supplanted by another useful incarnation.

5 | The Roosevelt Peace

POLITICAL DEATH is seldom decorous, and the decline and fall of the British Empire was comparatively swift and, to the British, deeply disconcerting. The stasis that afflicted the empire after the unification of Germany made possible the economic dominance of the United States. The shock of the Boer War suggested the limitations of British power, while the carnage of the First World War inflicted psychic, as well as political, wounds that have never fully healed. By the time the Germans were on the march in the late 1930s neither the British nor any of the allied powers in Europe were prepared to resist. The British declaration of war on Germany was late in the day, half-hearted, and accompanied by uncertainty. Britain went to war against Hitler to guarantee the independence of Poland, but it was helpless—then and six years later—to sustain its guarantee. France had been equally devastated by the war of 1914–1918 and was even more dangerously divided. The British sent an expeditionary force to France to await Germany's next move while its Cabinet pondered a separate peace or some manner of diplomatic arrangement with Hitler to avoid protracted conflict.

These were the ingredients that made the swift German conquest of France and the Low Countries possible, and pushed Britain into permanent secondary status. The Soviet Union was eager to make common cause with the Germans, both because Stalin recognized how vulnerable he was beside Germany and because it served Russia's historic cult of defensiveness. While Hitler's aggressive intentions toward the East may have been evident to any careful observer, Stalin was determined to ignore Russia's peril in exchange for the semblance of safety. These were the ingredients for the initial German dominance of the European continent, but this was also the opportunity that the Americans had contemplated since the turn of the century, and which Roosevelt was determined to exploit. With the surrender of France and the isolation of Britain in the summer of 1940, Roosevelt recognized that the United States had not only been afforded an opportunity to take its place among the great powers but could claim dominance far beyond anything Theodore Roosevelt and his nationalist brethren might have foreseen in 1900.

Roosevelt was, above all, an inspired pragmatist: he saw that principle coincided with power, and he was capable of expressing the aspirations of the American Century in idealistic terms. He knew that Britain could not sustain its colonial empire once its economic and political reserves were exhausted, but he couched this belief in the language of Wilsonian self-determination. Roosevelt may have disapproved of the idea of empire, but he also knew that the abdication of the British, French, and Dutch empires at the end of World War II would leave a vacuum to be filled by a bureaucratic empire, sewn together by treaties but administered from Washington. He understood that the military defeat of Nazi Germany was likely to lead to a semblance of German dis-unification—as it did for a half-century, by virtue of the division of Germany between Russia and the

West. It is difficult to discern what Roosevelt's fundamental attitude was toward Germany's place in Europe; but he did know that, within his own purview, Germany would be reduced to subordinate status for the foreseeable future. He knew also that European unity, while an ideal in itself for social and economic purposes, was not likely to lead to European political power, since no power in Europe— notably Germany, France, or Britain—was inclined to cede influence to any other state or collective bureaucracy. Nor was Europe capable of economic recovery on its own or, after three devastating wars in the 75 years since German unification, inclined toward military self-sufficiency. There was only one alternative, as Roosevelt knew.

We should not be led astray by Roosevelt's public piety about the United Nations Organization or his Tennysonian visions of a parliament of man. He saw the United Nations not as an extranational guarantor of the peace but as an instrument of American leadership which featured the additional attraction of aggrandizing the member-states without significant power. Thus, while Americans and the West might be impatient with the rhetoric emanating from the General Assembly, they must also recognize that the UN is just the sort of institution, by Roosevelt's design, to give the aggrieved powers of the world the illusion of significance. Roosevelt was a politician of such skill that he could sustain the Allies during the war against Hitler, and claim their gratitude, while reshaping the postwar landscape to favor American interests. In Britain's case this was made easier by the introduction, after Yalta, of a Labour government that was determined to do what any American government would have wanted it to: de-colonize, leaving those spheres of influence to the United States, and nationalize its economy to the advantage of American manufacturing and finance. The American victory in 1945 was so complete that the Europeans, by themselves, did what was necessary to yield to American dominance in the postwar world.

The singular exception, of course, was Soviet Russia. One might argue that while the cold war was the unavoidable consequence of the collapse of Hitler's Europe, the division of Europe between West and East was Hitler's gift to posterity. Europeans who look to the United States to find the origins of the cold war would do well to recall the circumstances that made the cold war inevitable. They were not America's doing, even if American policy had been designed to take swift advantage of the implosion of Europe. It is poignant to hear those British accounts of the Second World War, still often repeated, which describe Roosevelt's unsubtle slighting of Churchill at Tehran and Yalta in order to cultivate Stalin. Roosevelt made the mistake of suggesting to the British that his personal charm might be persuasive with Stalin when, of course, he believed no such thing; he knew enough of Stalin to know that such overtures were futile. Roosevelt did not seek to seduce Stalin at Churchill's expense; he sought to emphasize to Stalin that, no matter the condition of Britain and Western Europe, the United States was not prepared to cede the postwar world to Russian *diktat*, even if the Red Army occupied half the continent of Europe and was subsidizing anti-colonial movements in Asia. Among other things, Roosevelt recognized that Britain was, at best, a secondary factor in the coming postwar balance of power; he also knew that Stalin would someday disappear and that no successor was likely to inherit his status or influence. Thus, the long, slow decline of the Soviet Union began at the moment of its greatest influence. This does not mean that Russia ceased being a lethal threat after 1945—as the Ottoman experience would suggest, empires are frequently at their worst as they deteriorate—but it does mean that Roosevelt's promotion of a bipolar postwar world was, in the long run, well designed to challenge and ultimately undermine the Soviet Union.

In this light, Roosevelt's prosecution of the Second World War may be seen to conform to a pattern. Whereas his grappling with the particulars of the Depression was a series of gambles in the guise of "bold experimentation," designed to some degree to reform capitalism in order to save it from the excesses of socialism and laissez-faire, his determination after the French surrender was to project the United States into the European war while managing the gathering Japanese threat in the Pacific and positioning the United States to exert its influence to the fullest extent. In this he succeeded—at a relatively low cost in lives, and along with the recovery of American industry. After Pearl Harbor Roosevelt deliberately emphasized the European theater at the expense of the Pacific—although, with his customary sleight-of-hand, the British were mistakenly convinced that the United States Navy dominated American strategic thinking and that Roosevelt's primary focus was on the Japanese war. Lend-Lease put Britain in a permanent state of indebtedness to American power and largesse, and by delaying the opening of a second front in Europe until the Allies enjoyed sufficient material advantage, it was left to the Soviet Union, in Churchill's phrase, to "tear the guts" of the German army. Roosevelt was determined to maintain

American independence or dominance in any theater, and so was prompted to invade North Africa from the west in order to meet the British moving east against the combined German-Italian forces, and he initiated the defeat of Mussolini in Sicily. By the time a cross-Channel invasion was contemplated, one year later, it was self-evident that the United States would not only dominate the invasion force in terms of numbers, but would command its planning and execution as well. There would be no independent operations within some informal framework, as might have been the case in the First World War; despite some British feints in that direction—especially when General Montgomery sought to seize the initiative after the Battle of the Bulge—and the chronic difficulties of dealing with the French forces under General De Gaulle, the United States was more than first among equals in the West.

This may be seen not only in the organizational structure of the war's prosecution, but in strategic considerations as well. While the American invasion of Germany from the west was a deliberate affair, designed to destroy Germany's military capability, the British were anxious to gain ground and seize political objectives as swiftly as possible. This resulted in some misguided ventures, notably the airborne assault on Arnhem; but it also reflected the fact that while the British were running out of resources in the course of the war, the United States was in no particular hurry, precisely because it did not require the capture of political objectives (notably Berlin) and was content to let the Red Army bear the brunt of defeating Germany. This may have been cynical, as a matter of statecraft, and it could not have gone unnoticed by the Russians; but it accomplished American aims at minimal cost to the United States, and left the U.S. dominant within its sphere by the time of the German surrender.

When, in fact, Germany finally capitulated, Roosevelt had been dead for nearly a month, but the circumstances were essentially as he had preconceived them. He recognized, at Yalta, that the Russian–German conflict had redrawn the contours of political Europe and left a permanent division with which the United States and its democratic allies would have to contend. But that was the price of victory. At what point the victims of Stalin's westward movement would be liberated, no one was prepared to say in 1945; and Roosevelt recognized that he was presented with a military and political reality that was beyond his control. But the United States had not entered the war to guarantee the Polish borders, as Britain had done; Germany had declared war against the United States in concert with Japan, and the United States had prevailed by sustaining the British, sponsoring the French, liberating the Italians and northwest Europe, organizing the West to dismantle Hitler's empire, and pushing the Japanese back from China, Burma, Korea, the Philippines, southeast Asia, and the Pacific islands.

In that sense, of course, the decisive meeting of the British, Russians, and Americans was not at Yalta, which was essentially an anticlimax, or at Potsdam, which simply affirmed the reality of the cost of German surrender, but at Tehran (1943), where the coalition against Hitler was essentially divided between the interests of the United States and the ambitions of the Soviet Union. Roosevelt, like any democratic politician, was prone to dress his historic objectives in principled language, and so he conceived the Atlantic Charter, to codify America's common cause with Britain against Germany, as well as the United Nations, to administer a bipolar world in American interests—along with other similar nostrums and incantations. But while the Four Freedoms or the prayer he pronounced on D-Day might have appealed to the romantic strain in American statecraft, the fact was that just as Roosevelt had diagnosed the peril of Hitler in peacetime, he took advantage of the war against Hitler to maneuver the United States into global primacy. He might well have done this for the reasons that were often cited to justify American prosecution of the war: the defense of liberty, the assurance of American independence from dictatorship, the leap of faith required to defend American freedom at home by challenging tyranny abroad. But it is probable that he did it for the same reason most national leaders define their actions in terms of their interests: because he did not wish to expend the might and energy of his country in order to emerge from conflict in thrall to another power. Just as he was prepared to defend American power in the Pacific by the development of an atomic weapon, he was willing to supersede his senior partner in the coalition against Hitler, and to allow his ally of convenience to lose tens of millions of its citizens, to achieve American aims. Whatever principles such behavior might have represented, it left the United States the primary victor of World War II, an imperial power without an imperial structure, and the arbiter of the postwar world.

6 | "I am from Abilene"

Because today that dream of mine ... has been realized beyond the wildest stretches of my own imagination, I come here, first, to thank you, to say the proudest thing I can claim is that I am from Abilene.

Dwight D. Eisenhower, 1945

WHEN GENERAL EISENHOWER took leave of England in 1945 he was given the Freedom of the City of London, an archaic ritual that suited both the sense of what Britain owed Eisenhower and Eisenhower's feeling for the history in which he had participated. The opening thought of his speech of acceptance—"Humility must always be the portion of any man who receives acclaim earned in blood of his followers and sacrifices of his friends"—was characteristic of the soldier who hated war, but so was his recurrent theme: "I come from the very heart of America." Eisenhower was not just a product of middle America, removed by more than distance from the capital of the dying British empire, but a man who, by more than circumstance, had come to personify the American commitment to the war against Hitler—and in due course, the debut of American supremacy in the world.

Eisenhower's rise to power was not unprecedented, but ultimately it transcended his nominal role as the supreme commander of Allied forces in the Second World War and came to symbolize the global status of the American republic. Eisenhower's career had been a series of advances on merit: he did not come from a family with a military tradition—indeed, his parents were River Brethren, a pacifist sect—and his Army career had languished in the American twilight between 1918 and 1941. But he was the beneficiary of both the Army's capacity to recognize ability and the culture of a tiny officer corps that enabled him to stand out. When the United States retrenched after the First World War and the Army contracted in size, Eisenhower became the protégé of a general officer, Fox Conner, who helped to prepare him for the senior command Conner saw in Eisenhower's future. When the Germans invaded Poland in 1939, Eisenhower was barely a lieutenant colonel who had spent the previous four years languishing in Manila as principal aide to Douglas MacArthur in an ill-fated effort to create an independent Philippine army. But he was also on the short list of the incoming chief of staff, George Marshall, who had an eye for talent and the power to reposition favored officers, and rearrange the senior command, of an awakening peacetime army. In this sense, Eisenhower benefited from patronage, and it is probable that he would never have served as supreme commander had it not been for the sponsorship of Conner and Marshall.

But he did not prosper in a vacuum, and neither Conner nor Marshall took an interest in him out of charity. What they saw, in a younger officer, is what his London audience saw in 1945 and the American electorate recognized seven years later: a natural leader with the power to inspire as well as orchestrate, and a successful military statesman with the natural instincts of a politician and a wisdom born of experience. Experience tends to be an overrated virtue in politics, but in Eisenhower's case it was a decisive quality, married as it was to success.

To be sure, the world into which Eisenhower was born was very remote from the world he came to dominate. With Eisenhower, as with any public figure, it is difficult to discern the difference between the words he spoke and the thoughts he harbored; but there is little evidence that he did not mean what he said about the importance of Abilene, Kansas—to himself, and to the new American colossus of the mid-twentieth century. Abilene in 1890 was scarcely removed from its Wild West days, and although the Eisenhowers were members of a small-town middle class that was barely distinguishable from counterparts elsewhere in the country, they were nevertheless Westerners. Pennsylvanians of German descent, members of a small, characteristically German-American Protestant denomination, Eisenhower's parents were educated pioneers who chose to make a living on a frontier that still harbored hostile Indians and genuine cowboys and imposed considerable privation and isolation on settlers. Eisenhower's father was a conscientious householder and provider but not possessed of much ambition; he was a slightly distant planet in his son's universe. The primary influence in Eisenhower's upbringing was evidently his mother, the sort of pious matriarch who administered a household of six sons on limited means and impressed her offspring by example. In a community that was neither sophisticated nor genteel—a market town and way-station on the cattle drives—all six of the Eisenhower boys left the homestead and made successes of their lives.

Nor can it be said that Dwight Eisenhower stood out

from his brothers in any telling fashion. He was first among equals within his cohort, but so were several of his siblings in their time; he was a superior student, with a considerable competitive streak, and a voracious reader, but so were most of his brothers. This is not meant to suggest that Eisenhower's qualities remained dormant within him until later in life, or that luck plays the decisive role in historic ambition. But just as no one anticipated Franklin Roosevelt's future in his youth, nobody would have recognized in the young Dwight Eisenhower the historic figure he would become. There is a difference, however: in Roosevelt's case, this is because the affect of FDR's earlier life concealed the ambition that was clearly his; in Eisenhower's case, it is because he was only one of a multitude of smart, directed young men (and women) whose social circumstances mitigated against them. Whereas Roosevelt's formative years might be said to have been designed with something like the presidency in mind—as an only child of Hudson River gentry who was exhorted by the Reverend Peabody at Groton and excelled at Harvard—Eisenhower's prairie upbringing, humble family background, and passion for some practical livelihood motivated him more to overcome his material circumstances than to push himself toward special success. Eisenhower, like Roosevelt, possessed a complex interior life; but unlike FDR, Ike did not disguise this complexity behind an affable exterior but confined it within a stern simplicity. Like Roosevelt, Eisenhower was a sociable man, but it was a sociability that co-existed with an awareness of the exigencies of day-to-day survival that must have been alien to Roosevelt.

Two decisions that shaped Eisenhower's life and career

must be considered in light of this personal calculation. Doubtless Eisenhower's instinct for self-advancement must have been accentuated by his need to earn money between high school and college—and not just anywhere, but at the same place, an industrial creamery, where his father was employed. The deferral of his ambition can only have raised its intensity. It must also have impressed upon him the importance of avoiding the safe careerism that allowed his father to subsist, but not thrive. By the same token, after the interval of a few years, he sought admission to the Naval Academy as well as West Point not because he was generally convinced about a military career but because they offered a free education and, to holders of a commission, a beginner's entry into the higher reaches of the American social hierarchy. One hostile historian has referred to Eisenhower's "crafty . . . self-protective" nature, but craftiness and self-protection depend on a viewer's perspective. Eisenhower, the son of a yeoman household in a rural town of remote Kansas, can hardly be accused of cynicism when the upward path was so self-evidently steep. A man whose power derives from his native capability and personal ability to exude command may be excused a certain calculated intensity in life. And just as his contemporaries underestimated Roosevelt, Eisenhower's political adversaries misconstrued his exterior simplicity, his studied cheerfulness, as incapacity.

I have already mentioned the apparent charm of Eleanor Roosevelt that was fastened to her status as niece of the president of the United States. On a slightly lower pediment we can appreciate that Eisenhower saw in Mamie Doud of Denver not only the vivacious Army wife she became, but also the daughter of a comfortable, not to say prosperous, family that must have seemed comparatively grand to a second lieutenant from Abilene. In marrying above his station Eisenhower acquired not only the necessary family adjunct required by the singular rites of the officer class but a measure of wealth and social status that, in America's democratic culture, were instantaneously his. The Douds were not so well off that Eisenhower might have traded his living for the agreeable existence of the leisure class, but they added to Eisenhower's standing within the Army's social hierarchy and gave him a kind of journeyman status among those officers—George Patton being a notable example—who constituted the American equivalent of a military gentry. Would Eisenhower have thrived in the Army without Mamie Doud or, conversely, if he had addressed himself to his profession with the monastic intensity of a George Marshall? It is impossible to say; we only know what actually happened in his life, and cannot extrapolate anything beyond that. But it is not difficult to see the contours of Eisenhower's career in his determination to get out of Abilene, to go to West Point, to make the Army his career, and to marry the kind of woman who would advance his status.

And yet, in kicking the dust of Abilene from his heels, Eisenhower was the first to recognize that he was a product of that place, that it shadowed his progress in the Army, that it informed his ideals in ways he could and could not recognize—and that, a half-century later at the head of an American army in Europe, his status as a son of Abilene made him not just picturesque but romantic, in British eyes, and a potent symbol of the Anglo-American crusade against Hitler's Third Reich. The horrors of the European war, and in particular Germany's culpability, may have affected the

German-American Eisenhower more than he expressed publicly. But by the same token, he cannot have been unaware of the extent to which Abilene had shaped this descendant of German immigrants who had come of age in Kansas. As both Roosevelt and Eisenhower demonstrate, there are different ways to exemplify what it is to be an American. In Eisenhower's instance, we can accept his assertion that his Abilene origins were decisive. On a larger scale, however, they signified America's coming-of-age in the world, when warfare had upset the global order of power, the United States was no longer divided by region, and a plain-spoken general from the isolated—and isolationist—Middle West had become the symbol of American power and resolve in a fractured world.

DWIGHT EISENHOWER did not arrive at the United States Military Academy at the age of 21 with any long-range intention to make the Army his career. He came for the free education and for an opportunity to play for the West Point football team, which he did with conspicuous success until a debilitating injury put an end to his playing —and very nearly his military career as well. This seems to have been a singular blow to the young Eisenhower, deeply demoralizing, and the final two years of his tenure at the Academy were anticlimactic: his grades declined, his disciplinary infractions increased, and he developed a generalized sense of what we would now call alienation from the enterprise. In the end, he graduated in the low-middle range of his class—which, of course, was not an indicator of his intelligence or ability but rather a signal of uncertainty not unexpected in someone of his background at the Military Academy.

It was also emblematic of his lifelong ambivalence about the military profession: he understood and appreciated the business of being a soldier, but he chafed at the impudence of the parade ground and derided military pomp and circumstance. He relished command, studied power, and immersed himself in the details of official responsibility, but he was notoriously indifferent to decorations, uniforms, all manner of spit and polish, the surface etiquette and decorative side of military life. Eisenhower was famously hostile to inter-service rivalries and meaningless ritual; he deliberately shoved his hands in his pockets and kept his uniform decor to a minimum. His best-known contribution to military wear—the Eisenhower jacket of World War II—was a study in lack of pretension. To some degree this attitude derived from a native humility, all the more remarkable for being genuine, and to some degree it showed the streak of rebelliousness that kept him out of favor at West Point and prompted him to concentrate on poker at the expense of his studies. But it also reflected his commonsense tendency to separate the important from the unimportant in a business that is deadly by nature—and of fundamental importance to the life of the country he was sworn to defend.

Eisenhower may have been a disaffected youth in his mid-twenties, but he was not foolish, nor was he prone to throw away a unique opportunity: whatever purposelessness he may have felt after four years at West Point did not prevent him from undertaking the life of an officer with due seriousness. A year after graduation he married well, and a son was born the following year. But with this auspicious debut came frustration as well. Not only was he unable to secure an overseas assignment during World War I, he was prevented from obtaining any sort of troop command because the Military Academy wanted his services as a football coach. Eisenhower was a good coach, and a conscientious servant of an institution to which he owed a great deal, but he was deeply disappointed at missing the war in Europe and squandering his soldierly talents on the playing fields of West Point. But it was at this point—establishing a pattern in Eisenhower's career—that opportunity arose: in 1919 he was engaged in a cross-country military caravan designed to test the capacity of the Army to move troops and equipment around in the event of emergency.

As always, Eisenhower proved himself a superior officer, combining efficiency and ingenuity with a native affability. (The great trek "supposedly" impressed upon him the need for a nationwide road network which, four decades later, became the Interstate Highway System.) But with success came nemesis: in 1921, while he was stationed at Fort Meade outside Washington, his three-year-old son died of infection after a brief, agonizing illness, made even more poignant for his parents by the boy's enforced quarantine. It is impossible to exaggerate the effect of his son's death on Eisenhower, even in an age when child mortality was still relatively common. (It is pertinent to note that Eisenhower, Roosevelt (1916), and Winston Churchill (1922) all suffered the death of a young child within the space of a few years—a coincidence that would seem astonishing today.) It seems apparent that his wife suffered some kind of breakdown after the tragedy, and Eisenhower himself may be said never to have fully recovered from it. Forty years later, full of age and honors, he wrote that it was "the greatest disappointment and disaster in my life, the one I have never been able to forget completely"—an extraordinary assertion for an elderly man, separated from the event by two world wars and two terms in the White House. He commemorated the boy's birthday annually with flowers for his wife; and when he was very near his own death, during a cross-country journey from Gettysburg to California, he was seen to grow morose and agitated when the train passed in the vicinity of his son's grave.

While it is, as I have said, impossible to exaggerate the potential impact of this somber episode on Eisenhower, it is equally difficult to examine evidence that is implicit rather than explicit. Despite his lifelong diary-writing habit, Eisenhower's personal reflections, even at that stage in his career, have an impersonal quality that frustrates attempts to understand his interior life. Nevertheless, just as Roosevelt's polio, contracted in 1921, seems to have fortified whatever determination governed his soul, the death of Eisenhower's son in that same year appears to have had a similar effect on the prairie youth and debonair officer. Eisenhower may have fallen into the military profession by stages, yielding to it with a certain uncertainty and indecision, but after 1921 it is difficult to find any trace of ambivalence. Mamie Eisenhower retreated to her family in Denver and Eisenhower was soon assigned to the Panama Canal Zone, where he fell under the influence of that aforementioned senior officer, Major General Fox Conner, who not only recognized the singular abilities of his youthful subordinate but marked him as a future leader in the Army. Unlike General Marshall, who was similarly inclined to survey his fellow officers for signs of promise, Conner took it upon himself to tutor Eisenhower in military doctrine and to advise him with the explicit intention of preparing him for senior command.

The balance of Eisenhower's Army career, the decade-and-a-half between his exile in the tropics and the outbreak of World War II, is the familiar story of thwarted promotion and glacial evolution in the Army as an institution. At one point Eisenhower seems to have briefly considered the idea of resigning his commission and starting over in life—perhaps, in an uncharacteristically romantic idea, as an Argentine rancher—but apart from this brief episode, he retained his commitment to his career as an officer and prospered in his fashion. It is striking to note that, after the early 1920s, Eisenhower was universally recognized as one of the more promising officers in the Army, and that he took advantage of each opportunity and preferment that came his way, excelling at the Staff and Command School and otherwise continually educating himself for higher command. And yet, because of the temper of the times and the microscopic size of the Army, his efforts were poorly rewarded. As he entered middle age he was still a comparatively low-ranking officer; as a major in his mid-forties, he was not likely to reach the upper echelons before enforced retirement.

Nevertheless, the experience he accumulated in middle life proved, accidentally or not, to be especially pertinent to his later career. He alternated between service on the American Battle Monuments Commission in Paris—which gave him an intimate view of European politics and affairs, and earned him the patronage of the commission's nominal chief, General John Pershing, who was also (in retirement) the Army's most prominent and influential public figure—and in the War Department, which educated Eisenhower in the folkways of political Washington. It did not transform him into an Army bureaucrat, of whom there were altogether too many in the comfortable officer class of the 1920s and 1930s, but it afforded his perceptive eyes a close-up view of the way the Army worked, its relations with Congress, and the ways things got done (or undone) in the political capital. There is a famous story, told by Harry Truman in his dictated memoir, that the outgoing President Truman felt compassion for the incoming Eisenhower, who was accustomed to the Army and so would presume that he could snap his fingers, in his White House office, and get instant results. This shows not just a misunderstanding of military life—as Truman, a Reserve Artillery captain and war veteran, should have known perfectly well—but a keen misunderstanding of Eisenhower. Because he had dealt with the Army, as a junior officer, from a senior officer's perspective, and had been eyewitness both to success and to failure—most notably in his service as General Douglas MacArthur's chief aide during the Bonus Army debacle (1932)—Eisenhower was more aware than most of the limitations of command, and knew as much as Truman about the machinery of government in Washington. It was Eisenhower's singular political skill to disguise a subtle understanding of these matters behind the bland exterior of an agreeable, capable officer.

It is this subtle political skill that explains the next two formative episodes in Eisenhower's long preparation for senior command. When President Roosevelt declined to appoint General MacArthur to a further term as chief of staff, in 1935, MacArthur was invited to the Philippines, in irregular status, to organize and train a Philippine army in preparation for independence—and, implicitly, for the possibility of conflict with Japan, which Roosevelt anticipated with the steady militarization of the Japanese government. MacArthur recruited Eisenhower as his deputy, and Eisenhower, with some misgivings, accepted the assignment. The source of those misgivings is not difficult to discern: while the Philippine enterprise was, to some degree, a unique opportunity for a perceptive officer, it was also virtual exile from the centers of power and, to a lesser degree, would put Eisenhower in MacArthur's shadow and orbit. MacArthur was a famous, one might say notorious, figure in the Army and in the national imagination; but he was also a controversial officer out of favor with the Roosevelt administration. The Philippines, moreover, were no longer the experiment in enlightened despotism that William McKinley envisioned but an American colony that the United States did not wish to retain and was planning to liberate. The value of the Philippines assignment, from Eisenhower's perspective, lay in the opportunity to closely observe the construction of a national army, and to gain a rare perspective on the Pacific theater. This was to prove invaluable to Eisenhower later, when General Marshall, by then chief of staff, instructed Eisenhower to concoct a strategy for the defense of the Philippines against Japan; but that was a happy accident. In the mid-1930s Eisenhower is more likely to have seen Manila as a stage for advancement through proximity to an Army mandarin, by way of building and training an army from scratch, in the principal overseas possession of the United States.

Of course, as we know in retrospect, things turned out rather differently. MacArthur, always jealous of talented subordinates, did little to encourage Eisenhower's ingenuity or loyalty; and Eisenhower, for his part, saw clearly the extent to which he and MacArthur differed as officers. Eisenhower, said MacArthur in later years, was "the best clerk I ever had." Eisenhower, for his part, once said that he had "studied dramatics" under MacArthur. In fact, both benefited from the association in ways they may not have recognized. MacArthur enjoyed the luxury of having the most promising officer in the Army as his deputy, gathering around himself the sort of mystique he liked to cultivate as an American proconsul in the Pacific. Eisenhower not only sharpened his craft as a writer, drafting MacArthur's pronouncements, but got to know the business of dealing with strategic allies and foreign governments at first hand. And while he may have believed, at the time, that his tenure in Manila was squandered, it also kept him distant from the toxic military politics of Washington in the late 1930s, when an isolationist Congress was in conflict not only with the Roosevelt White House but with the military establishment in general. It was, from the standpoint of an ambitious officer, a good time to be distant from the center of things, and to be a symbol of useful endeavor, not endless intrigue.

That positioning, in turn, brought Eisenhower to the fuller attention of General Marshall, who was to prove to be his most consequential mentor, and who was still quietly taking notes on the state of the Army. Of course, anyone who becomes a general officer and, at the most decisive moment in modern American history, chief of staff, is not likely to be entirely without personal ambition. But it is fair to say that Marshall's primary interest was in building an Army that would be equal to the task he saw ahead, and in understanding the Army he inherited in 1939 with an eye to swiftly expanding its size and multiplying its quality. Marshall was an officer of uncommon learning and sagacity, but he was also a talent-spotter who had a unique ability to anticipate the needs of an army in a European war and to match them with officers he had observed and tested. The

War Plans division he established at the War Department was the most important venue in American preparations for World War II, for two reasons: first, it operated on the assumption that American military involvement was inevitable, and would be far more diverse in nature and global in scope than the expeditionary force of World War I; and second, it served as a training ground, and baptismal theater, for the future leaders of the war. Marshall, who had been promoted by Roosevelt to chief of staff without regard to seniority, was equally indifferent to archaic claims of promotion or preferment: he tolerated the manifold eccentricities of officers like Patton or MacArthur, who had sought to blight Marshall's career, while cultivating the careers of younger officers of very different character but equal promise: Eisenhower, foremost, as well as Omar Bradley, Henry Arnold, Lucian Truscott, William Simpson, Matthew Ridgway, and innumerable others.

By the time of Pearl Harbor Eisenhower had long since returned from the Philippines and had recognized that the gathering emergencies in Europe and Asia were likely to propel him to high command. Marshall, accordingly, assigned him to senior staff positions in Texas and Washington state, and could hardly have failed to observe Eisenhower's superior performance in the massive war games in Louisiana in the summer of 1941. Summoned to the War Plans division and charged with mapping out a defense of the Philippines, Eisenhower was not just swift and perceptive in his work but sufficiently confident to argue with Marshall and gain his confidence. Despite his lack of direct combat experience and relative paucity of troop commands, Eisenhower presented to Marshall as a specimen that was new to the

American military tradition: a soldier-diplomat who was uniquely fitted for warfare among allies in a conflict that threatened the foundations of Western democracy.

In considering what sort of general officer should lead American armies in a second World War, Marshall recognized that Eisenhower was singularly, perhaps uniquely, equipped for the task. A soldier who had studied military science in dense detail, an experienced officer equally at home in the field and in the corridors of the Department of War, a diplomatic warrior who combined a will to prevail with the personal qualities of leadership, Eisenhower had risen, of his own accord, from the middle of America to the center of world events at the moment his country needed him most.

8 | Soldier of Democracy

EVERY PROLONGED WAR has the effect of clearing out the senior generation of general officers to make room for younger commanders, and World War II was no exception. In the Soviet Union, of course, Stalin's purges of the officer corps in the late 1930s produced this effect in exaggerated fashion; in the British Army, after May 1940, Churchill's relentless—some would say capricious—series of reorganizations of his senior command did yield, in the end, such superior officers as Harold Alexander, William Slim, Alan Brooke, and Bernard Montgomery. Eisenhower was an obvious beneficiary as well: George Marshall had become chief of staff on the day that the European war broke out, and Marshall, who had himself been pushed past dozens of claimants to the head of the line, had maintained a list of potential commanders since long before he was in position to act on his instincts. Eisenhower was not first among equals at the beginning of hostilities, however: he was only one of many languishing officers—a lieutenant colonel—who seemed likely to excel and had been marked for possible high command.

Eisenhower, however, had other virtues that matched the needs of the Army during that period between the time the United States assumed something like a war footing and when mass numbers of troops were committed to action.

Observing Eisenhower in the War Plans division assured Marshall of Eisenhower's intellect, powers of organization, and independent mind; it also revealed Eisenhower's diplomatic—one might even say political—skill along with his professional ability. Accordingly, Eisenhower's first major assignment was in London, as commander of American forces in Europe at a time when there were no American forces in Europe. The task consisted largely of acquainting himself with the theaters of war—a talent he had mastered in the Philippines and used to good effect in Marshall's War Department—and personifying the American war effort in Britain.

In this, of course, he was famously successful. Thereafter the British often complained that American strategy favored American interests and imposed American leadership; and General Patton, for his part, complained that Eisenhower was "the best general the British have." It is tempting to conclude that these diametric reactions prove that Eisenhower succeeded at his diplomatic assignment, but they also reveal the depth of difficulty he encountered. The British, having stood alone against Hitler for over a year, and now engaging the Germans and Italians in North Africa, looked upon their new American comrades roughly as they and the French had greeted the Expeditionary Force in 1917: they saw themselves as tutors to the Americans. Eisenhower, having listened to General Pershing's recollections in the 1920s, was prepared to avoid playing such a role. In one sense, Eisenhower was better equipped than Pershing had been: American entry in World War I had been notably reluctant, and Wilson and his secretary of war, Newton Baker, imposed limitations on Pershing's freedom of action that did not apply to Eisenhower a quarter-century later. This is not to say that Eisenhower was given a free hand, or was not mindful of General Marshall and his civilian patrons in Washington; but he had their confidence to a much greater degree than Pershing would have recognized, largely because the task at hand was so much more desperate. No one in the United States in 1917 assumed that a loss in Europe would threaten the freedom and independence of Americans; in 1941 such a possibility was altogether real.

Eisenhower did not come to Europe as a subordinate American but as a harbinger of things to come—as he and his more perceptive British associates (including Churchill) understood. It was clear that the war against Hitler was destined to exhaust the resources of the Empire and leave even a victorious Britain in a vastly reduced state in the world. It was equally clear that the gaping power vacuum that a German collapse, Britain's exhaustion, Russia's supreme sacrifice, and European disorder would yield was to leave the United States in a position of primacy very nearly unprecedented in modern history. This was, of course, even before the United States developed the atomic bomb in 1945, giving it absolute strategic mastery, and before the Soviet Union developed its own atomic device four years later, yielding the cold war. Eisenhower, as much as any officer, recognized that circumstances were going to force an end to the historic isolationism of the United States and demand not just American participation in the global conflict but American leadership as well. The difference is that, while Eisenhower believed in the global mission of the United States and was as eager as Roosevelt to seize the opportunity, he was more than a reflexive nationalist or political opportunist. We may assume, since he often said so, that he saw the United States and its practical power as an instrument to do good in the world; but he also saw that American power was best exercised in tandem with like-minded powers, and that the kind of system he would seek to create in the postwar world would rest on a series of interlocking alliances, a web of mutual respect among democracies which the United States would guide, and sometimes lead, but not necessarily dictate.

This was what Eisenhower, in his presidential years, meant when he would talk about the spiritual leadership of the United States: a power and authority grounded in respect as much as deference. To be sure, this was an ideal that was, just as often, observed in the breach—his vision of the usefulness of the United Nations was probably as cynical as Roosevelt's—but it was an ideal to which Eisenhower consistently aspired, and which has generally informed American policy since the end of World War II.

As the senior military commander of the senior partner in the Allies' war against Hitler, Eisenhower was, of course, the supreme diplomat-general of the war. But he was more than a bureaucrat, or the stumbling ambassador of the pact with Vichy's Admiral Darlan, or the friendly face of American power in the European theater. It was Eisenhower who made the basic military decisions that were meant to realize the political objectives of the war, and it was Eisenhower who, at two critical moments in the conflict, forced the tactics that proved decisive in victory. Eisenhower had begun as a kind of liaison between the United States and the British war effort: he was the American who cultivated the British military and political establishment, and then advised his masters in Washington—that is to say, Marshall, Roosevelt, and the secretary of war, Henry Stimson—about the war as he saw it. Eisenhower's geniality and gift of conciliation were critical, but his powers of observation, and his cold calculation about the conflict at hand, were supreme. Eisenhower was therefore able to translate American intentions into terms and conditions that the British could tolerate; similarly, his prestige, which was based on both authority and character, allowed him to adjudicate matters between the Allies, among senior American commanders, and between the Allied forces and the American political leadership in Washington.

He was not only personable but effective and indispensable. No American, before or since, had ever exercised such decisive influence abroad on behalf of his country; and it is fair to guess that no American general—with the possible exception of Marshall—had wielded such power with such political skill. Marshall swiftly recognized this, of course, as did Roosevelt, which in turn prompted Roosevelt to retain Eisenhower in the field while keeping Marshall to himself in Washington. Apparently it was Marshall's ambition to lead the invasion of France, and there was even some bureaucratic movement to the effect that Eisenhower might yield his command in Europe to return as chief of staff to Washington and make room for Marshall; but it is impossible to imagine that Roosevelt ever seriously contemplated giving up Marshall's immediate service, on which he had grown dependent, though it would have been entirely characteristic of Roosevelt to lead Marshall (and, in turn, Eisenhower) to believe otherwise as suited Roosevelt's purposes. When Stalin demanded some specific assignment of command for

Soldier of Democracy

a second front, FDR's hand was forced, and his choice was Eisenhower.

He made this choice, undoubtedly, for several reasons. First, he wished to keep Marshall in overall command of the war effort, and Eisenhower was in a position where he was not only conspicuously successful but familiar to the British and well-regarded by the Allies. Also, he recognized in General Eisenhower something of the qualities that made Roosevelt a supreme politician and consummate war leader: a gift for command and authority, coupled with a genial temperament and an unblinkered eye for his country's interests. Eisenhower was full of elevated ideas—"I'm idealistic as hell!" he once exclaimed in Algiers to an astonished British minister-resident, Harold Macmillan—but he was without illusions, too. He saw the conditions under which the British sustained their war effort, and was simultaneously sympathetic and perceptive; he saw the extent to which the disorder of global conflict demanded American intervention, and he maneuvered to make that possible. In addition, Eisenhower had not been unnerved by the dread responsibilities that had fallen on him. He not only maneuvered in London and Algiers and Gibraltar with authority and political finesse, but he extricated himself from complicated circumstances: his pragmatic decision to cooperate with the Vichy government in North Africa had appeared naïve, but in the fullness of time it proved prescient—and, with Darlan's assassination, produced the stroke of luck that seems every successful politician-general's birthright. Moreover, when American troops, in their initial engagement in North Africa, were handily defeated at the Kasserine Pass by General Rommel's Afrika Korps, Eisenhower swiftly moved to execute a change

71

of command, found the right officers to solve the problem (Patton, Bradley), and showed no evidence of loss of nerve.

Eisenhower's resolve in the fortnight before the invasion of Normandy, especially his decision to delay the deployment of his armies across the English Channel because of the weather, only sending them in at the critical moment, is justly celebrated. But another episode better represents Eisenhower's capacity as a commander under the harshest conditions. That would be the German offensive in the west in the week before Christmas 1944, which became known as the Battle of the Bulge. In one sense, it could be argued that Hitler's gamble was made possible by Eisenhower. Because Eisenhower understood his orders to be to destroy the German war-making capacity—rather than seizing what he regarded as political objectives, such as Berlin—he was induced to pursue a methodical, and relatively slow, broad-front strategy, which extended the Allied lines beyond their safe capacity to contain German penetration. Add to this the bitter winter weather, and the German attack enjoyed the twin elements of surprise and disorganized resistance. The Germans were able to exploit weaknesses in the long Anglo-American front, and Eisenhower was caught sufficiently off guard to find himself in the greatest peril of his career.

Yet it was a peril which contained, as Eisenhower immediately recognized, opportunity as well. To be sure, his British colleagues, notably Montgomery, and to a lesser extent the American army commander Patton, were impatient to gain ground and invest cities at the expense of destroying the German army; but it should be understood that the British sought what they glimpsed to be a swift end to the war because they needed the war to end quickly. The American army, as Eisenhower knew, was in no such predicament: the Germans were hard-pressed on their eastern front, and the Allied air forces were methodically destroying their ability to make war in the west. Time was on the side of the Allies, not of the Germans (or the British), and Eisenhower was determined to use that time to destroy the German military and ensure that a prolonged resistance, or postwar guerrilla campaign, would be unwelcome and impossible. It should also be said that, while historians are prepared to argue about the virtues of a broad-front strategy versus a pointed campaign aimed at the German capital, it is by no means certain that the capture of Berlin would have ensured a German collapse or prevented further German resistance—any more, indeed, than having German armies virtually at the gates of Moscow had deterred the Red Army from resistance and retaliation. In the Bulge, therefore, Eisenhower may have been surprised, but he was scarcely stymied: he saw that the sudden and dramatic exposure of German forces within the confines of his own lines gave the Allies an unexpected opportunity to methodically isolate and defeat the Germans. He saw, as well, that he had no other responsible choice in the matter: a substantial Allied reversal, at that juncture, may not have jeopardized the outcome of the war but certainly would have prolonged it.

In the midst of this tactical drama, of course, Eisenhower had to deal with Montgomery's demand for temporary authority during the Ardennes offensive, an assumption of control which Eisenhower, not unexpectedly, regarded as unlikely to be temporary and which, at any rate, was clearly insubordinate. And yet, in this instance as well, he reacted in a way that both affirmed his own mastery and avoided a fatal confrontation with Montgomery. His signal to his masters—Marshall, Roosevelt, and Churchill—to choose between him and Montgomery could be answered in his favor only, as he knew; but he delayed its dispatch to give Montgomery's faithful deputy General de Guingand time and opportunity to explain to his chief his untenable predicament and for Montgomery to gracefully withdraw the challenge, save his command, and maintain the harmony of the Anglo-American alliance. This, in its purest form, was the Eisenhower technique at war: swift action to ensure the success of any individual enterprise, combined with political skill and personal finesse that left few scars or wounded feelings among friends and inflicted maximum injury to enemies. Montgomery himself all too readily perceived Eisenhower's talent for converting internal discord and ostensible disaster into progress, all while maintaining his good offices and deploying his personal charm—which might help to explain Montgomery's subsequent combination of deep personal affection and smoldering professional jealousy for his wartime superior.

9 | The Monarch of the Glen

IT IS A FAMILIAR complaint that Americans have a weakness for electing war heroes to the presidency, but it's a complaint without much foundation. George Washington might be described in such terms, but that would underestimate what Washington meant to the new republic, especially after the Constitutional Convention. In the nineteenth century there were only two generals who moved in swift succession from the battlefield to the White House— Zachary Taylor and Ulysses S. Grant. Dwight Eisenhower might reasonably be described as a "war hero," and it is certainly true that he would never have become president without his service as supreme commander of the Allied forces in World War II. But the precise circumstances of his election are often forgotten, at some expense to understanding his significance.

In fact, World War II was seven years in the past when Eisenhower was elected in 1952, and this interregnum tells us as much about Eisenhower as it does about the convergence of forces that propelled him into the White House. Eisenhower did not quit the Army at the end of the war; he succeeded Marshall as chief of staff, presiding over the dismantling of the wartime force. He was chief of staff during the period when the services were integrated into the Department of Defense—and, notably, when the Army was racially desegregated. When he did, in fact, retire from the Army, it was during a year (1948) when he was under considerable pressure to run for president. No less than the incumbent president, Harry Truman, as well as FDR's eldest son James Roosevelt, implored him to seek the Democratic nomination in a year when the Republicans, who controlled Congress for the first time in two decades, were expected to reclaim the White House. Eisenhower privately declined the invitation and publicly disclaimed political ambition, citing his status as a professional soldier in a democratic system—which might explain Truman's subsequent animus toward him. Instead, he chose to become president of Columbia University and write his wartime memoirs.

He did not, however, divorce himself from the Truman administration, and he maintained a semi-official portfolio as an adviser to the national military establishment, which included consultations with Truman, Secretary of State Dean Acheson, and senior officials in the burgeoning postwar national security apparatus. This period of transition from a wartime footing to a loose grappling with the growing implications of the postwar world was not the "return to normalcy" that had governed American foreign policy after 1919 but the birth of the Pax Americana that would dominate world affairs into subsequent generations. This was not fully understood at the time—as the swift transition to a peacetime military footing would attest—but Eisenhower comprehended the practical outcome of the war, and the gradual development of an apparatus to support America's new status and responsibilities bears his imprint. It should not be forgotten that when Churchill, involuntarily retired from power, described in March 1946 the "iron curtain" that had fallen across the frontiers of central and eastern Europe, dividing the communist east from the democratic west, his words were not entirely welcome and, to no small degree, were resented by those who did not recognize the fundamental shift inherent in the defeat of Germany and the rise of Stalin's Soviet Union—or, perhaps, welcomed the balancing influence of a communist empire against the Western democracies. Eisenhower felt a sentimental attachment to those Russian comrades who had dismantled the Wehrmacht on the eastern front, thereby making his victories possible, and he was always a reluctant warrior; but he was neither blind nor self-deluding, and understood the fundamental nature of the Soviet system. Eisenhower had been an advocate for the new Central Intelligence Agency, and he recognized, as well, that the consolidation of the armed services and the creation of a new Department of Defense were fundamental to America's new responsibilities.

Above all, Eisenhower believed in the efficacy of strategic alliances—not because he wished to subtract from any American contribution to keeping the peace, or considered the exercise of American power to be illegitimate without collective sanction, but because he thought that united democracies were a more formidable obstacle to Soviet expansionism, and because he believed that the Europeans, who had been demoralized after the First World War and were essentially prostrate in the aftermath of the Second, needed to be given a stake in the gathering conflict between East and West. If this meant American patronage as well as sacrifice, so be it: Eisenhower believed that the practical assistance inherent in the Marshall Plan, combined with American pledges to Western European security, were essential to keeping the peace. That is certainly why he joined the argument on behalf of the Truman administration during the debate over the North Atlantic Treaty Organization in 1949, and why he took leave from Columbia in the following year to return to Europe and assume the military command of NATO.

All of this coincided, to some degree, with the outbreak of hostilities on the Korean peninsula, which distracted attention from Eisenhower's activities as the uniformed symbol of the American commitment to Europe. But while the cold war was playing itself out in one theater directed by his old patron/rival MacArthur, Eisenhower was in the other theater supervising the construction of the postwar settlement, which was to obtain for the subsequent four decades and which remains essentially in place today. Eisenhower, the general who presided over the conquest of Nazi Germany, now stood as the American bulwark defending Western Europe against Soviet communism. It was at this time, of course, that George Kennan in the State Department posited his famous "containment" doctrine, which was based on his understanding of Russian provincialism and defensiveness. But Eisenhower, whose knowledge of Russian history might not have been as deep as Kennan's, saw things that Kennan failed to notice: namely, that while Russia had always felt historically isolated and frustrated in the councils of Europe, and the horrors of the German invasion had furnished a rationale for Russian insecurities, there had always been an evangelical component to communism as well, and Stalin would not hesitate to extend the zone of Russian influence wherever possible—even beyond Russia's historic "near neighborhood." Moreover, while Soviet communism was aggressive as well as defensive, Western Europe was not immune to Soviet blandishments and would naturally resent the sudden American hegemony that guaranteed its freedom. Eisenhower believed in fighting the cold war because he understood the absolute stakes involved, but he believed in fighting it on an ideological, as well as military, front. The United States, in his view, was required not only to hold the line against Soviet expansionism but to define the terms of the cold war for Europe—and, in due course, for those non-aligned states that had no immediate stake in its outcome. In short, Eisenhower believed in the power—the essential power—of propaganda; and in dealing with an adversary that was determined to thwart the flow of information, he strongly advocated those measures—a robust intelligence establishment, broadcasts to Warsaw Pact populations, cultural exchanges, and education—that would fight the cold war by political means. As president, he conflated federal patronage for undergraduate and postgraduate education with the "national defense" because he believed that the two ideals enjoyed a symbiotic relationship.

These, then, were the circumstances that compelled Eisenhower to seek the presidency in 1952. As a personal matter, at age 62, having operated at the highest levels of national service for more than a decade, he would have preferred to retire; but from NATO headquarters in Paris he, better than anyone else, was in a position to understand that the cold war was not a distant conflict that could be safely monitored from afar, and that the outcome of every presidential election was critical. As a Republican, he had his differences with the Truman administration and had become convinced that the Democrats' two decades in power had proved corrupting; but the decisive element in his decision to run was the likely nomination of Robert Taft by the Republicans.

It is periodically observed that the Republican party is riven by factions which threaten to pull it apart, but the truth is that there have always been conflicting strains among Republicans—no less than among Democrats—and that in the absence of unifying leaders like Roosevelt or, in later decades, Ronald Reagan, the two parties are subject to varying influences. In a nation the size of the United States, in a system that features two prominent political parties, it is hardly surprising that there should be intra-party differences among Democrats and Republicans; but this seems to come as a revelation to every new generation of students of American politics. It is equally true that there are moments when these differences within parties are of historic importance, and in 1952, the future of Republican foreign policy was at stake. Taft, an impressive intellect and a skilled parliamentarian, was the avatar of the GOP isolationist wing— an ironic turn of events, as he was also the son of William Howard Taft, an "internationalist" by the standards of the early twentieth-century party. But Robert Taft had not only been an isolationist before Pearl Harbor, he remained so after 1945, and he had been a stalwart opponent of the creation of NATO. It is amusing to recall that one of Taft's ancillary points was that American troops were likely to remain stationed in Western Europe for years to come, an assertion that was stoutly disputed by NATO proponents. But Eisenhower was indifferent to the matter: he considered the projection of American power in Europe not just critical to keeping the peace, and insurance for American security, but a small price to pay for what he considered an essential investment. Taft may have won that argument on points, but it was (and remains) an irrelevant argument.

Eisenhower believed not only that the Republican party would be imperiled if Taft prevailed, but that the course of American foreign policy was likely to drift from the chart that he, among others, had mapped out if Taft were to become president. As a practical matter, the Democratic nominee in 1952, Governor Adlai Stevenson of Illinois, who had served in the Roosevelt Navy Department and in the Truman administration, was far closer to Eisenhower than to Taft in his world-view; but Eisenhower was genuinely disturbed by the domestic policies of the Truman White House, and Stevenson was the favorite son of his party's center-left wing. It did not take too much effort for Henry Cabot Lodge, grandson of the namesake who had argued successfully for amendments to American participation in Wilson's League of Nations, to promote an Eisenhower candidacy and, finally, to persuade Eisenhower to resign from the Army, return home from Paris, and seek the presidency.

Eisenhower's two terms as president are an interesting study in the exercise of power, partly because he famously deployed his power as much by indirection as by decree—the "hidden-hand presidency"—but also because he was commander-in-chief at a unique moment in the American imperium. During the 1950s the existential threat from the Soviet Union receded, especially after the death of Stalin, which occurred a matter of weeks after Eisenhower took office; but the West was still in recovery from World War II, and the debate about the Korean conflict in the Security Council had revealed the basic weakness of the United

Nations as a decisive factor in world affairs. Eisenhower, like Roosevelt, believed in the ideal of the UN; but it was a belief observed in the breach, and premised on the notion that the work of the United Nations should coincide with the strategic interests of the United States. Europe, too, was equivocal at this time. The devastated condition of the continent required an unprecedented act of diplomatic philanthropy in the form of the Marshall Plan, but restoring European institutions, as well as the physical structure of cities and (it may be argued) the morale of the population, was a long-term undertaking. Hitler invaded Poland before Europe as a culture had fully recovered from the wounds of the Great War, and the vast, unprecedented destructiveness of the 1939–45 conflict had only exacerbated Europe's trauma. It is possible, of course, that the American mission to Europe created a passivity and dependency in Europeans which has, in later decades, become a chronic problem in American diplomacy; but this is a risk that Eisenhower did not foresee or, if he did, considered secondary to the urgent requirements of American policy in the early cold war era. Simply stated, Eisenhower not only personified the American umbrella over Europe but, from his position of unprecedented strength and prowess, directed the course of transatlantic policy and remained first among equals in the democratic resistance to the Soviet Union and its subordinate states in the Warsaw Pact. No president had directed American policy with such unilateral discretion before, and none has since.

Eisenhower was confronted with two equally daunting challenges: preserving the peace in the presence of an adversary newly in possession of nuclear arms, and guiding the American public toward global leadership. This was no small matter: the United States had traditionally kept itself removed from global politics, and until the twentieth century its army had been employed for the unique tasks of preserving the union in civil war and pacifying the frontier west. There has been no period in which American nationalism coincided with imperial ambition, and it has required political leadership to accustom the American public to the rigors, and the necessity, of global responsibility. That had been Roosevelt's aim, beginning in the late 1930s, and it was Eisenhower's mission as the soldier-statesman of the 1950s to affirm an American commitment to the preservation of peace and the defense of freedom overseas. But whereas FDR had contended with the traditional powers in Europe and an expansionist Japan in Asia, Ike was obliged to contend with an aggressive adversary that not only sought to subvert American interests but possessed a reserve arsenal of nuclear weapons. Accordingly, Eisenhower considered it his duty not just to protect American interests and guarantee the freedom of Western Europe, but to do so while striking a diplomatic balance with the Soviet Union that would prevent a nuclear conflict. From the perspective of the twenty-first century, we see the peril in the proliferation of nuclear weapons and the access to nuclear technology by irregular forces, but in the mid-1950s these were only gestating threats overshadowed by communist power in Europe and, after 1949, in Asia.

Eisenhower also inherited a domestic mood that required political skills of considerable sophistication. Fear and uncertainty about communism had accorded considerable power to Senator Joseph McCarthy, whose behavior Eisenhower rightly considered to be inimical to long-term American interests. His decision to subvert McCarthy by degree and reassert his authority within his own party was carried out by avoiding direct confrontation (a tactic which had failed to work for Truman) and persuading the public that Eisenhower, not McCarthy, was the wise guarantor of American security. It was also Eisenhower's lot to deal with a Congress which, after 1954, was controlled by Democrats but which proved largely compliant on those issues that he considered important. Indeed, the Democratic leadership in Congress did not challenge Eisenhower on any serious level in foreign policy until relatively late in his presidency, and then only (on the question of the "missile gap" with the Soviet Union) in the context of the 1960 presidential election, in which Eisenhower might have been an issue but was not a candidate. Eisenhower had campaigned in 1952 on an ambiguous promise to "go to Korea" and get a soldier's assessment of a war in perpetual stalemate; that he did so, and indeed forced an armistice within a few months of taking office by secretly threatening the use of tactical nuclear weapons, shows the sort of maneuvering that was characteristic of his confidence. Just as he had threatened to resign his command in 1944—knowing that his putative rival, Montgomery, would be the commander compelled to quit—so he maneuvered the recalcitrant North Koreans into accepting his specific prescription for an end to hostilities. This had the salutary effect of instituting an acceptable status quo on the Korean peninsula, as well as solidifying his reputation among the allies and satisfying American public opinion.

No president before Eisenhower wielded such authority across the global landscape, and no president since has enjoyed the freedom of movement, or the capacity to influence events, that Eisenhower did during the eight years he presided over the reconstruction of Western Europe and the remapping of the global landscape for the balance of the cold war. By the swift and certain deployment of Marines in Lebanon in 1958—and their equally swift and certain withdrawal—he exerted his influence in a Middle East that was no more receptive to being dictated to then than it is now. And by choosing to stand in defense of the tiny nationalist Chinese redoubt on Formosa he kept the People's Republic of China at bay and demonstrated to our onetime adversary, and now ally, Japan the resilience and fidelity of American power. Eisenhower was a believer in the missionary power of American ideals; he used words as weapons as readily as he used armaments. And while his presidency was not an unbroken series of triumphs—there was the misdirection of the 1956 Hungarian revolt, and the mortification of the U-2 affair in 1960—such reversals were, in the broader scheme of a world in conflict, comparatively minor events without lasting consequences.

THE EISENHOWER PRESIDENCY was bracketed by two ironies. The first occurred in 1952, when Eisenhower inaugurated his campaign in Abilene by complaining about the potential for waste and abuse in military spending. This was followed by his observation the following year, as president, that "every gun that is made, every warship launched, every rocket fired signifies, in the final sense, a theft from those who hunger and are not fed, those who are cold and are not clothed. . . . This is not a way of life at all, in any true sense. Under the cloud of threatening war, it is humanity hanging from an iron cross." This from a man who had chosen the profession of arms as his livelihood, had acquired what stature he enjoyed by commanding vast numbers of troops in war, and who had launched his campaign for the presidency from the literal front line of the cold war, at NATO headquarters.

Eisenhower left office feeling discouraged. The Paris summit conference of 1960 had collapsed in disorder in the wake of the U-2 affair, when an American reconnaissance plane was shot down over Russian territory, and his scheduled visit to the Soviet Union was canceled by the Soviet government. Nor did the election of John Kennedy as his successor ease his burden of conscience, since it implied a repudiation of his policies, and he considered Kennedy a novice with no real appreciation of the perils and potential of the presidency. And yet, in the course of a world tour in the same year that Kennedy was elected, Eisenhower was greeted by appreciative, even rapturous, crowds in such places as India and Pakistan—indeed, in both Pakistan *and* India—where he spoke to audiences estimated in the millions. The fact that his political capital was vastly diminished in his homeland—the Democrats had built on their commanding majorities in the House and Senate two years earlier—even while his prestige abroad was never greater must have struck Eisenhower as mystifying, at the least.

And yet, in both these contradictions, we may find something of Eisenhower's enduring strength as a leader. Like most soldiers with experience of war, Eisenhower found little to romanticize about it: "I hate war as only a soldier who has lived it can, only as one who has seen its brutality, its futility, its stupidity." Eisenhower was not a romantic personality to begin with; he was the least likely general to find fulfillment in military theater. He might well have understood what Oliver Wendell Holmes meant when Holmes talked about "the soldier's faith" in his Memorial Day address at Harvard, but Eisenhower would have been puzzled by Holmes's sense of having been morally instructed by war. Eisenhower had the democratic professional's attitude toward war in the sense that he had mastered the military art in order to serve those who made the political decisions about war, but this was just business to Eisenhower, not personal conviction. He possessed a Kansas Republican's view of defense spending as a cruel necessity but not something that was sacrosanct in itself, or immune to the stewardship of good government. Just as he felt compelled to warn his callow successor about the political challenge inherent in a "military-industrial complex," he was equally persuaded that "every gun that is made" might well be produced at the expense of the things that make life worth living.

It is all too easy, however, to misunderstand Eisenhower in this regard, to assume that he believed something that he did not. His regret that guns must be manufactured and wars fought—or his view that the intertwining of industrial capitalism and national defense demands the vigilance of taxpayers—does not mean that he failed to recognize the dread price of freedom and prosperity. There is a difference between the citizen's expectation that funds for defense be spent wisely and the conclusion that funding defense is a waste of resources. Eisenhower hated war and its cost to civil society, and he avoided it to the extent that he was willing to gamble with nuclear weapons in order to outmaneuver his country's adversaries; but he did not believe in the avoidance of war at all costs, any more than he approached the Soviet Union in an importunate mood at the summit. Eisenhower not only preferred to bargain from strength, he sought an overwhelming advantage. Just as he gambled with his command in December 1944 without really gambling, so he invited the Russians to the summit in 1955, and again in 1959, when it was the Soviet Union, and not the United States, which sought a reduction in diplomatic tension. Eisenhower preferred to remain the senior partner in any bilateral negotiation, which is why this scourge of the military-industrial complex expanded the size of the armed forces, commissioned new generations of weaponry in the Army, Navy, and Air Force, tested atomic weapons, threatened the recalcitrant North Koreans with tactical nuclear bombs, and commissioned a secretary of state who practiced "brinkmanship" with a nuclear-armed Soviet Union.

Indeed, not only did Eisenhower strive to achieve American mastery in the cold war, he sought to ensure that every Western undertaking bore the American imprimatur. The basic design for this conception may be found in Eisenhower's enthusiasm for strategic alliances. With the United Nations, his policy was twofold: in those situations where the interests of the United States were, at best, problematic —most notably, African decolonization—he was happy to allow the UN to take the lead in supervising what was necessarily a disorderly and unrewarding process. In those other instances where the interests of the United States were directly involved, or where the cold war threatened global stability, Eisenhower was pleased to adopt Roosevelt's vision of the UN as an instrument of American power. Just as the mandate of the United Nations was useful to the United States in the 1962 Cuban missile crisis and the 1991 Persian Gulf War, Eisenhower's prestige was such that he could orchestrate the policy of the UN toward, for example, the 1956 Hungarian revolt—although he understood the fundamental meaninglessness of UN pronouncements in such instances, as well as the limitations of American (or NATO) action.

This approach was most dramatically illustrated in the 1956 Suez War, when it fell to Eisenhower to precipitate a crisis in Anglo-American relations, and to wound the British government of Anthony Eden, in order to establish—or re-establish—certain principles that Eisenhower believed were important to consecrate. It may well be that Eisenhower was genuinely distressed by the clandestine Anglo-French-Israeli operation after Egypt's nationalization of the canal, fearing the consequences for the supply of oil to the United States, Western Europe, and Japan, as well as the blow to Western prestige among the Arabs at a time when the Soviet Union and the West were competing for influence in the Middle East. But it is likely, as well, that the Suez operation offended two presumptions that Eisenhower considered to be of paramount importance: the importance of timing in international affairs and the strict necessity of consultation with the United States. The Suez crisis broke out as the Soviet Union was in the midst of suppressing the Hungarian revolt, and on the eve of the American presidential election. Eisenhower could not join in the Western condemnation of the Russian invasion of Hungary at the same time that Western powers were employing force to reclaim a canal within Egyptian territory. As much as Eisenhower decried the unilateral Egyptian seizure of the canal and must have mistrusted Gamel Abdul Nasser, he was equally persuaded that such undertakings must be guaranteed to succeed. This was the instinct of the gambler who held all the cards, as Eisenhower always sought to do, and the fear of someone who knew the potential cost of failure. Eisenhower, as president, would never have sanctioned the successful 1954 coup in Guatemala, or the equally deft 1953 restoration of the Shah to the Iranian throne, without the certainty of success. For the British and French to have conspired without recourse to American guidance (and in alliance with Israel) against the principal Arab power struck

Eisenhower as misguided. In his view, whatever temporary success may have been achieved by the invasion of Suez came at the cost of permanent American interests, in the Middle East and elsewhere.

Of course, Eisenhower's angry reaction to the Suez affair ultimately cost Eden the premiership, an outcome the United States scarcely welcomed; and while British opinion was divided on the venture, there was considerable public anger in Britain at the United States. And yet Eisenhower looked at Suez, as he tended to regard such events, in the long term. Whatever administration was destined to succeed Anthony Eden—as it happened, it was led by Eisenhower's wartime colleague and confidant Harold Macmillan —would act swiftly to restore good relations with the United States, understanding the relative stature of Britain and the United States in the world. At a moment in history when Great Britain was divesting itself of the remnants of empire and adapting, with mixed success, to the postwar industrial economy, no British government was in any position to act in defiance of the stated interests of its principal ally and patron. This was a hard lesson for the British to absorb, but one that Eisenhower, by force of reputation, was capable of teaching while maintaining, by force of personality, the historic ties between the United States and Britain.

In this sense, of course, Eisenhower was unique: Franklin Roosevelt had dominated circumstances because he was president at the moment when the United States fully accepted its global responsibilities; but Ike was, by himself, symbolic of American power in ways that FDR was not. This is not to suggest any fundamental disparity between the achievements of the two but, instead, to emphasize the extent to which American dominance in world affairs had expanded by the 1950s.

At the same time, it was not in Eisenhower's nature to appear in the guise of the colossus that the United States had actually become, or to operate in explicit pursuit of American power and influence. The "hidden hand," in that sense, was employed in the creation of the multiple alliances that Eisenhower and his indefatigable chief diplomat, John Foster Dulles, promoted around the world: mostly in imitation of the structure of NATO—down to their comparable acronyms, like SEATO and CENTO—and all designed to give lesser powers and strategic allies a sense of shared responsibility and the protection of American power. Eisenhower designed these garments with the goal of defending democracies (or strategic allies who may or may not have been especially democratic) against the encroachments of communism, especially in the Middle East and Asia. But their purpose went beyond the gamesmanship of Soviet-American competition outside Europe; they signified, as much as anything, that the United States was the pre-eminent power in the West, and by any practical measure the most powerful nation on the planet.

After the collapse of the Soviet Union, in 1991, it was said that the end of the cold war, and the end of the bilateral rivalry between the United States and the Soviet Union, left the world with only one "hyperpower," in the French formulation. The presumption behind this assertion was that, since the end of World War II, there had been two main powers of equal strength and durability in operation. But that was not true by the time the Berlin Wall was dismantled, nor had it ever been true. The United States and the Soviet Union were never equally matched, by any measure: the economic power of the United States was always superior, and the strategic and military resources of the United States could not be duplicated by the Soviet Union. Even if other communist powers—notably China—were added to the equation, there was no comparison, partly because the United States still outranked the communists in measurable qualities and partly because China and the Soviet Union were very nearly as antagonistic to each other as either was toward the United States. After 1943 there could be no question of the dominance of what Churchill, two years earlier, had called (in explaining the Atlantic Charter to the British public) "the most powerful state and community in the world." The Soviet Union possessed a substantial military establishment, and ruled by force of terror and intimidation in the old Russian empire and in eastern and central Europe. But the strategic isolation of Russia remained profound, and its capacity to project what power it possessed was always limited. It might even be said that there was something poignant in Russian patronage of Cuba, or about the post-colonial communist regime in Indochina, especially since (North) Vietnam was effectively stalemated by its proximity to China, and even so tentative a chief executive as Kennedy was able to intimidate the Russians successfully when they installed offensive missiles on their subservient Caribbean isle.

Eisenhower was always aware of this imbalance, and his understanding of American power, especially in relation to the Soviet Union, was always predicated on the American doctrine of putting an overwhelming preponderance of resources behind the use of force, or the threat of force. To be sure, Eisenhower was easily disconcerted by domestic political attacks, especially late in his tenure, on American capacity or preparedness: he knew, as he once explained, that American power was "awesome ... [and] respected elsewhere"—which was to say that the Soviet Union had a candid knowledge of the relative power of the two rivals, even if certain Democratic senators did not. But his strategic actions as president, and his view of the postwar world, were informed by a confidence not only in the quality of American power—that is to say, the country's social, cultural, and moral resources—but in the ability of that power to sustain itself and defend its own interests while also protecting America's friends and allies. That is why Eisenhower invested as much as he did in the war of ideas—exporting American political doctrine and culture—as in military armaments. These efforts may have been naïve, and might not be practical in present circumstances; but it could be argued that the multitudes that responded to Eisenhower abroad were not just grateful for American hegemony but for the example of American ideals as well.

Nevertheless, while Eisenhower had a clear understanding of the relative power of the United States and the Soviet Union, and was correspondingly sanguine about the ultimate outcome of the cold war, he knew as well that the weakness of the Soviet Union could make it dangerous in ways that required special vigilance. The Russians, after all, possessed nuclear weapons, missionary fervor about Marxism-Leninism, and, at mid-century, the ideological allegiance of a certain portion of the world's intellectual class. This distinction between absolute power and the simple capacity to do great harm is especially evident to Americans in the age of terrorism, when nuclear weapons or chemical and biological agents might well become available to ideological or religious antagonists. One might argue that Eisenhower discerned the dangers of the Soviet Union more readily in smaller increments: in the wars of ideas in Asia and Latin America, in the struggle for control of oil in the Middle East, in the subversion of the will to defend democracy and resist communism in Western Europe. Eisenhower, accordingly, was an especially generous patron of his intelligence agencies, relying on them not only for information and comprehension but to carry out the secret missions that supported the larger strategic interests of the West, and to counteract Soviet espionage, which did not strain Russian resources but yielded them considerable benefits and was more successful in the West, and in the United States, than we may care to admit.

The irony, if that is the word for it, is that Eisenhower seldom expressed himself in such terms; he considered it his responsibility as president to assure, rather than alarm, Americans, and to speak in idealistic, not strategic, terms when defining American interests. This was Eisenhower the soldier who hated war, and regretted the necessity to build swords as well as ploughshares; and this was Eisenhower the statesman who expressed more faith in global bureaucracies such as the United Nations than he genuinely had. At a moment in American history when American power was supreme, and personified by one who represented both experience and judgment, Eisenhower dominated the world—to the extent that such dominance is possible—as no other president. The world he bequeathed to his successor did not change in an instant, but the quality of American leadership did change, and the world was subtly transformed. Eisenhower had not invited Nikita Khrushchev to the United States in order to assuage the Soviet leader's sense of rivalry, or to expose him to the variety of American national life: he sought to domesticate Khrushchev as a way of assuring Americans that the power of the United States was such that it could confidently entertain its dreaded rival without concern about the temporary consequences. If public opinion was relieved by seeing Khrushchev at Disneyland, or playfully arguing with selected Americans, then that was fine with Eisenhower. Ike understood how the game was played, he knew the score, and he enjoyed the kind of serene confidence that few politicians know, which allowed him to let his actions speak for themselves.

Epilogue

I

MARTIN GILBERT records Winston Churchill's despair in 1922, just after Lloyd George's wartime coalition had suddenly collapsed and Churchill was turned out of office. In notes for an election speech, Churchill laments the "disastrous events" of the new twentieth century:

> *We have seen in ev country a dissolution,*
> *a weakening of those bonds,*
> *a challenge to those principles,*
> *a decay of faith*
> *an abridgement of hope*
> *on wh structure & ultimate existence*
> *of civilized society depend.*
> *We have seen in ev part of the globe*
> *One gt country after another*
> *Wh had erected an orderly, a peaceful*
> *A prosperous structure of civilized society,*
> *relapsing in hideous succession*
> *Into bankruptcy, barbarism or anarchy.*

Addressing the future, Churchill warns:

> *Can you doubt . . .*
> *as you survey this somber panorama,*
> *that mankind is passing through a period marked*

Epilogue

not only by an enormous destruction
& abridgement of human species,
not only by vast impoverishment
& reduction in means of existence
but also that destructive tendencies
have not yet run their course?

These are curious words to have been written at the high tide of the Jazz Age, when the collapse of the old order seemed to have ushered in a new world that featured, in F. Scott Fitzgerald's formulation, "all gods dead, all wars fought, all faiths in man shaken." And yet, of course, they may be read as prescient, for the barbarism that had gripped Europe during 1914–18 had not been forgotten, the hopes that the postwar world invested in collective security were forlorn, and the "destructive tendencies" that haunted Churchill's thoughts had already taken root in Russia, were gathering in Italy and Germany, and were shaking the foundations of French, and to a lesser degree British, political culture.

Of course, we know how this chapter of the story ends: the furies that had gripped Europe on the Western Front were never wholly suppressed, and the 1918 armistice was broken by the Germans. The centrifugal forces that seemed to tear Europe apart—the swift capitulation of France, the isolation of Britain and its strain across the globe, the "total war" between Teuton and Slav on the Eastern Front, the destruction of the Jews under German occupation—did not succeed so much in settling the issues that had perturbed European diplomacy at the turn of the century as much as they exhausted Europe into quiescence. The onset of the cold war put Europe into suspended animation; and the eventual collapse of the Soviet Union did not herald a European renaissance so much as reawaken those dormant historical forces that the cold war had superseded. To adapt the journalistic phrase of the time, it was not the end of history so much as the resumption of history: the Balkans fell into rampant disorder, the Russian empire contracted and battled along its borderlands, the reunified Germans accepted their eastern boundaries with a measure of reluctance, the British seemed poised between America and Europe. The rebirth of the old League of Nations in a European Union seemed to thrive only so long as it restricted itself to economic and commercial issues. Strained by the outbreak of tribal warfare along its edges, and Muslim resentment within its borders, the EU seemed, at the end of the twentieth century, rather less than what its architects had intended.

Which is to say that, at the end of the cold war and the dawn of the twenty-first century, the locus of economic and military power in the world remained where it had been since the dawn of the twentieth century: in the United States of America. This is not to say that the United States exercised absolute authority in the world, any more than it had in the past: China's enormous size and potential loomed, as always, but the sleeping giant of Chinese economic and political power had been a figment of the world's imagination for decades—even for centuries—and it never quite seemed to awaken. By the end of the twentieth century the People's Republic of China had evolved from the world's largest communist system into the world's most populous fascist power, staging a kind of uniformed capitalism that kept its restive population under police supervision. The Europeans still constituted a significant portion of the global economy, and such emerging democratic nation-states as India seemed destined to gain influence in the global economic balance.

But none of this amounted to anything like a serious challenge to American primacy, or to the Pax Americana which had held since the end of Second World War. The American economy remained vital and resilient, and only the United States possessed the kind of concentrated military power—not to mention the will to use it—upon which the peace of the world was dependent. The American economy, like any free-market system, was subject to the vagaries of the business cycle, and the mood of the American society seemed curiously vulnerable to the seasonal fluctuations of the economy, as if recession or the creative destruction inherent in capitalism were somehow unnatural occurrences. But the American political system, at once dynamic and sclerotic, reactionary and imaginative, remained invulnerable to radical challenge, and retained its capacity for reform and corrective action.

The problem, to be sure, is that American power was never so great as anyone imagined it to be, or so pervasive. The United States in its time had won all its wars but lost many battles. The Soviet Union, which had challenged American hegemony, ultimately collapsed of its own weight in taking on a burden that it could not sustain. Neighborhood irritants such as the ambitious communist regime in Cuba did not constitute a sufficient threat to require remedial action. The war in Indochina had limited strategic importance and was prosecuted without conviction. American influence in the Middle East was complicated by allegiance to democratic Israel and dependence on oil. Efforts to engage post-communist Russia were equally complicated by its ambiguous relation to Western Europe, as well as by resurgent Russian nationalism. The Chinese were both dependent on American patronage and resentful of American power and Chinese impotence. All of these factors, taken together, seemed to suggest the "abridgement of hope" and "destructive tendencies" that had harried Churchill's thoughts a century earlier. But were they harbingers of worse to come, or the natural order of things?

The truth is that the Pax Americana has been no more comprehensive in its time than any other system of power. The Romans did not control the entire known world of their time, and they knew it: the centers of countervailing power were just too distant to engage, and of course, the barbarians subsisted on the other side of the forest. The British empire was largely a commercial enterprise, held together by a formidable navy but much too disparate to exercise anything like central authority, as the British themselves were aware. American power is similarly decentralized, and in many instances, the challenges to American hegemony in certain parts of the world are not sufficiently important to address in full measure. The United States should have no intention of wasting its resources in punishing Latin American irritants, or in chasing down petty tyrants in Africa. It is more than enough for the United States to understand and defend its own interests around the world, since, in the postwar scheme of maintaining the peace of 1945, it has also fallen to the United States to guarantee that peace.

The challenge is that the exercise of such power, the

assumption of such responsibility, is not a natural instinct among Americans. This is a society enlarged by immigration—and by the "manifest destiny" conceived to accommodate such immigration. Just as Americans have been reluctant to search the world for demons, they have tended to regard their global responsibilities as temporary assignments, reluctant undertakings with distinct beginnings and definable ends. Americans habitually insist on an "exit strategy" when they must surely realize that an "exit" may not be possible, and certainly is no part of any strategy to protect the national interest. The imperium over which America presides, the power that the United States has exercised, the global leadership that America has practiced, the peace that America has guaranteed, have been accomplished by a series of incremental steps, measures that filled a dangerous vacuum in the world but were largely in defiance of the basic instincts of Americans as global citizens. Americans are not naturally isolationist in the sense that they prefer to ignore threats to their own well-being, but they often have to be persuaded that such threats exist, that economic power and geographical distance are limited advantages, and that the cost of the maintenance of peace, and the protection of American security and interests, may be difficult to calculate—indeed, may be beyond calculation.

II

American leadership in the world has always been dependent on the vision of certain individuals, on the convictions, agitation, and political talent of those who have recognized that history makes certain demands on the United States

and that the cost of ignoring historic challenges is consider-
ably greater than any temporary sacrifice. This has been
self-evident since the middle of the nineteenth century,
when the economic power of the United States was beginning to be realized and the old structures of global power—
the empires and spheres of influence—were coming under
strain. By the time the United States chose to challenge the
aging Spanish empire in 1898, the outlines of this new reality were in sudden and dramatic relief: the United States
had had a much more difficult time keeping its own political
structure in order three decades earlier than it did pushing
the Spanish out of the Caribbean and western Pacific. Even
then, though, in the course of subsequently suppressing the
Philippine insurgents, it was evident that the exercise of
power was not without prolonged costs, and that the burden of power would be measured in years, not months; but
by choosing only to pacify the Philippines—and Haiti and
Nicaragua in the next two decades—rather than impose an
arbitrary sovereignty, the United States demonstrated that
curious combination of power politics and state idealism
that would distinguish it from the old colonial powers and
characterize its particular notion of war as an extension of
politics.

It may be argued that the weakness in Woodrow Wilson's
argument for war in 1917 was not strategic but tactical. He
understood the necessity, at that late stage in the Great
War, for decisive American intervention. But he clothed his
calculus not in the defense of American interests, as Theo -
dore Roosevelt had urged him to do, nor in the use of American power to alter the shape of European politics, but in
philosophical abstractions which may or may not have

applied to American security and certainly failed to appeal to the imagination of the American public. The stated reasons for American participation in World War I—to punish German transgressions of American neutrality and to make the world safe for democracy—were legitimate, to be sure, but they failed to define any fundamental American interest in the war's outcome. The Europeans had not gone to war over democracy, and the United States had tolerated considerable strains on its neutrality—including the mass killing of American civilians at sea—without recourse to war. Naturally, when the fighting ended—or, to be more precise, when the armistice was concluded—there was a general sense at home that the Germans had been suitably punished, and that the future of European democracy was again, properly, in European hands. Wilson's proposed League failed to attract the allegiance of Americans because it represented Wilson's equivocal vision of an ideal universe in which the United States may or may not have had a stake. There were, of course, those Americans who recognized the League's potential as a staging area for increased American influence in the world, and this prescience was scarcely confined to any one faction or party: indeed, those Republicans who supported American membership in the League against Senator Henry Cabot Lodge's reservations—William Howard Taft, Elihu Root, Henry Stimson, Charles Evans Hughes, and the other founders of the Council on Foreign Relations mentioned before—would remain committed to the vision of America as a world power.

Nevertheless, while American diplomacy has always benefited from the guidance of those convinced of such a vision, the American political system requires executive leadership—especially because, to paraphrase Wilson, "it is a fearful thing to lead this great and peaceful people" to global power. That is why Franklin Roosevelt and Dwight Eisenhower are such decisive figures in this argument: they embraced what they recognized as the historic responsibility of the United States in world affairs, they guided America into global dominance, and they personified, in words and in action, what American power meant for the peace of the world.

In a superficial sense, it is difficult to imagine two more dissimilar men. Roosevelt, the easygoing product of the old American squirearchy, who regarded political power and prerogative as his birthright, and Eisenhower, the industrious son of German Midwestern stock, who entered the Army for the free education and whose professional career was a series of uphill steps—these two men could hardly be expected to have much in common, or much mutual sympathy. But in fact, both recognized that the course of their lives coincided with their country's coming-of-age, and both were propelled by a singular ambition to overcome adversity, to excel, and to command. Both succeeded in disguising this ambition, and the cold calculation of professional and personal advantage, behind affable exteriors and oblique personalities. One seemed complicated, on the surface, and the other seemed simple; but the engine of their ambition was the familiar machinery of American life, and the circumstances that brought them together—positioned, as they were, at the center of events in the middle of the world's severest crisis—were not entirely coincidental. Both had been heading toward mastery of their respective realms as the United States, in the course of World War II, was swiftly and irrevocably being propelled toward the global preeminence that had so far only beckoned.

To be sure, while the two were roughly contemporary—Roosevelt was eight years older than Eisenhower—Roosevelt had understood his inheritance, and pondered his country's future, for much longer than Eisenhower when the two encountered each another. When Eisenhower was still a prairie roughneck, Roosevelt was observing his distant cousin's military exploits in Cuba from the vantage point of Groton School, which deliberately sought to inculcate its students with the ideal of public service. Eisenhower was still a West Point cadet, more adept at games than at cultivating senior officers, when Roosevelt was the Secretary of the Navy's conniving assistant. When Eisenhower was beginning to attract attention as a capable junior officer in the Army, Roosevelt was his party's nominee for vice president. Thereafter, however, both entered on a prolonged (and to some degree, calculated) period of preparation: Eisenhower in strategic service overseas and in the War Department, in the somnolent peacetime Army, and Roosevelt during his recovery from polio, as he struggled to maintain his status in New York state and national politics.

Roosevelt was a practiced politician for whom rhetoric was not just an essential component of his livelihood but indeed second nature. Eisenhower was a capable writer, a careful craftsman of words, but his was a military sensibility, in which words were to be deployed to practical ends and rhetoric focused on conviction rather than eloquence. Roosevelt knew that he wanted to exercise power and planned out the means by which to realize his ambition and justify his profession of politics, while Eisenhower simply pursued professional advancement and did not grasp the implications of his own position, and the slow American advance toward war in 1939–41, until relatively late. Yet when these two trajectories intersected—with Roosevelt leading the nation at war and Eisenhower becoming the face of the American war effort in Europe—they complemented one another so well that Roosevelt and Eisenhower became inseparably symbolic of their country at war and charted a course for the American imperium which still obtains.

Roosevelt's great contribution to his country's coming-of-age was twofold. First, at a time in the West when the prospects for democracy were dubious, and when the United States, by statute, was deliberately precluded from playing anything other than a supporting role in European power politics, Roosevelt, by his energy and rhetoric, demonstrated that democracy remained a vital force in the world, and that the radical causes, far right or far left, that were engaging the liveliest minds on either side of the Atlantic were worse than illusory. Roosevelt did not end the Depression, nor did he grasp the dimensions of the governing apparatus he had created in response to the Western economic emergency of the 1930s. But he did possess the successful democratic politician's capacity to translate the problems of the Depression into comprehensible terms, and he maintained the appearance of action throughout a period when appearances were the only real weapons at his disposal.

Roosevelt's other contribution was to recognize, early

and emphatically, the fundamental challenge to American freedom in the turmoil of Europe. He may have been contemptuous of Mussolini and baffled by Stalin's Russia, but he had no illusions about Hitler's Germany and its implications for the United States. Roosevelt comprehended the threat that Hitler posed not just to the peace of Europe, but to the long-term prospects of democracy; and he understood, especially at moments when his countrymen seemed determined to ignore what they could see, that it would fall to the United States, in a second "foreign" war, to resolve the imbalance of power in Europe, as it had in the first war. It is also probable that Roosevelt saw opportunity as well: Europe's disorder would leave it in disarray, and just as 1918 had provoked the sudden collapse of the old political order, the expense of a second war would exhaust the powers of Britain and France and their waning empires. Into this vacuum Roosevelt was determined to march, and long before the final outcome of the war, the primacy of American power—American industry for war manufacturing, the American economy and its financial resources to underwrite a war, American military strength to force its conclusion—was a fact of life. This did not result in an immediate reshuffling of the deck—unlike the sudden collapse of the European royal houses and imperial networks in 1918, the process of dismantling the British and French empires was prolonged, and the German attack on Russia created a countervailing power in Eastern Europe; but by the time Roosevelt died in April 1945 there was no question that Western Europe would emerge grievously wounded from its wreckage while the United States would move from secondary status in the world's councils to preeminence.

Eisenhower's contribution was of a different order, but it was no less decisive. It was Eisenhower who had presided over the military defeat of Nazi Germany, and he personified the substance of American power in Europe. He deployed his words as carefully and deliberately as his weaponry: by expressing common cause with democratic Europe, for example, or by his famous declaration, after touring one of the German concentration camps, that while he realized that not all American soldiers might understand what they were fighting *for*, the evidence of brutality and genocide would demonstrate what they were fighting *against*. Eisenhower was a potent symbol of the new American engagement in the world, but he was also a designer of the system and, at NATO, an active participant in the twilight struggle between West and East. When he became president, Eisenhower inherited a stable system of global alliances, ripe for growth, and an American commitment to sustaining the peace; but he also confronted a world newly traumatized by the spread of nuclear weaponry and an American society disconcerted by the substance and shadow of communist subversion in the United States. Eisenhower considered it his responsibility to take such action as was necessary to demonstrate that such dangers were manageable, and that the borders of the bipolar world of the cold war would be stable.

Eisenhower's prestige was such that he could settle the Korean conflict with a credible strategic threat and a commitment to compromise on the division of the Korean peninsula. Eisenhower also perceived that the death of Stalin, which followed closely his own accession to the presidency, would change the nature of the Soviet regime and, to some degree, the character of the Soviet threat. He knew that there would be a protracted internal struggle to reorganize power within the Kremlin, and he also knew that the strategic capacity of the Western powers—and especially the United States—exceeded the ability of the Soviets to practice aggression. Within the Soviet empire itself, first in East Berlin in 1953 and then in Hungary in 1956, there was open rebellion; and within the larger communist realm there was little unity, and much discord between Russia and China. Between his careful stewardship of American military strength and his well-informed assessment of Soviet capacities through intelligence, Eisenhower understood the relative positions of West and East and had the confidence to ease public tension and relieve anxiety by seeking accommodation with the Soviet Union at the summit—a meaningless gesture, in a strategic sense, but politically pertinent. Eisenhower enjoyed the trust of his countrymen and the confidence of the world in the midst of peril, because he not only projected a sense of command but neither overstated nor understated the stakes of the cold war. He did not exaggerate issues that he considered transitory—the status of Formosa's offshore islands, or the state of Lebanon's civil government—but he did not permit such problems to fester, or allow minor irritants (the Castro regime in Cuba, Indian non-alignment) to become major tests of American prestige.

In both Roosevelt and Eisenhower personal ambition was, by steady degree, transformed into public confidence, and neither hesitated to act on behalf of what they perceived as American interests. Both were ambitious for their country, and at certain strategic points in their presidencies, accustomed to act without regard to what they would have regarded as transitory political conditions. Roosevelt conducted war by stealth against Germany in the North Atlantic, and was content to manipulate—indeed, to mislead—public opinion if it served what he regarded as a larger purpose. Eisenhower's nature was not the same as Roosevelt's, but he was prepared to gamble with nuclear weapons and to use his clandestine services to achieve aims he, too, regarded as essential to American interests, whether in defense of the hemisphere against communist subversion or to preserve the supply of energy to the industrialized world. It would not have occurred to either to approach foreign powers, especially adversaries, in an importunate posture; and because their belief in the American capacity to preserve the peace was fundamental, they would never have felt an instinct to apologize for American power, or hesitated to deploy American power in defense of the peace. Both spoke the language of diplomacy, and neither projected the image of an insular or arbitrary power; but both protected their country's interests by leading, rather than following, public opinion and, as a matter of routine, by rewarding allies and punishing enemies.

III

Henry Luce, in his famous essay on the American Century, did not envision the primacy of American power in his time; he assumed that it was a fact, but wondered about the state of the nation—or the mood of the people, as he might have expressed it—in the face of global responsibility. That was in 1941. He thought that the United States was about to embark on war largely by accident, or inadvertence; he did not think that Americans fully understood what was meant by democracy or national security; he feared that once the defeat of Germany was accomplished—there was no mention of Japan since this was before Pearl Harbor—there would be an expedient retreat from world affairs. For whatever partisan instincts he may have harbored, he wanted Roosevelt to succeed in establishing the United States as a world power, indeed as the preeminent world power, where Wilson had failed.

In retrospect, Luce's concerns were not misplaced, although things have turned out rather differently than he anticipated. The United States became actively engaged in World War II not because of the increasing tensions between this country and Germany but because we were the victims of a sudden surprise attack by Japan on our western periphery. The United States declared war on Japan before Hitler declared war on the United States. In that sense, the Japanese attack on Pearl Harbor clarified what had been an ambiguous posture for more than two years, and by a combination of happenstance and Hitler's sense of obligation to his Axis ally, the United States fully entered the war on the side of the British, along with the remnant of General De Gaulle's French forces, the "free" governments of German-occupied Europe, and China, which had been at war with Japan since 1931.

The world was in some state of armed conflict throughout most of the 1930s, and since the end of World War II, Americans have lived through a series of crises and peremptory and long-term challenges that have featured their sustained military commitment to the defense of Western Europe; the defense of the status quo on the Korean peninsula; the deployment of American troops in dozens of locations around the world; a network of bases and military installations and a global armada of naval vessels, military aircraft, and space satellites; and combat in places as disparate as Korea, Central America, Indochina, the Arab peninsula, the Balkans, and Asia Minor. This is an impressive, and in some respects startling, legacy of the First and Second World Wars, and it is emblematic not only of the supremacy of American power but of the American commitment to preserving the peace. In one sense, the two world wars were concluded, but have never ended.

In another sense, it could be argued that our recent history represents a failure of American statecraft: if we measure success by the absence of conflict, or reduction in armaments, then we have not progressed very far since 1945. But this ignores the fundamental historical lesson of politics: that peace is preserved by preparation for war, and that war is precipitated by weakness, not strength. It would be obtuse to maintain that democracy under arms has betrayed the promise of American life: under the protection of the garrison state that has underwritten the Pax Americana, we have witnessed unprecedented developments in science, prosperity, human rights, scholarship, and the elements that nourish human freedom. It is true, as Eisenhower said, that every expenditure for armaments constitutes a theft from civil society; but it is equally true that American power, and the defense of American power, has not only protected civil society but allowed it to flourish in ways that were unimaginable during Eisenhower's lifetime.

Nor is this achievement confined to the material life: we are no closer to utopia today than at any other time in history, but it is difficult to survey the political landscape of the world without some measure of satisfaction. The United States can no more eradicate Russian nationalism, or Chinese petulance, or tribal enmity in the Balkans or in the Middle East, than it can alter human nature; but the United States, in concert with its allies, did precipitate the collapse of the Soviet Union, which, in turn, eradicated the balance of terror between East and West, and liberated the populations of central and eastern Europe. Now, as often happens in history, we recognize that with the disappearance of one overriding danger there can arise comparable perils in ancillary realms: today, in the rise of Islamist ideology, and in the proliferation of nuclear weaponry not only among hostile powers, such as North Korea or Iran, but among irregular forces as well. Their capacity to do harm may be limited, at this time, but we cannot be in doubt that they mean to do harm.

It is the fate of the United States, in its tenure as a world power, to be forever at strategic crossroads: whether to isolate itself from the conflicts of inter-war Europe; whether to embrace Roosevelt's vision of a United Nations under American leadership; whether to stand against communist aggression in secondary regions; whether to expand Eisenhower's purview to "bear any burden" across the world; whether to withdraw American troops from Western Europe; whether to spend the "peace dividend" that came due at the end of the cold war; whether to respond to the terrorist attacks on America in 2001 by destroying the perpetrators. And in fact, American policy since 1945 has been governed by a rough consensus but varying practices. The Republican party, which was the principal exponent of isolationism in the 1930s, is now generally committed to global engagement and the aggressive defense of American freedom and interests. The Democratic party, under the leadership of Roosevelt and Truman, designed the structure of the Pax Americana but has, since the Vietnam War, been ambivalent, at best, about the necessity of global engagement, and has embraced a form of appeasement in dealing with hostile powers. Neither of these postures are necessarily permanent, but it may be said that they represent the two divergent strains in the American engagement with the world.

The irony is that we have, in Franklin Roosevelt and Dwight Eisenhower, two dissimilar figures in American life and politics who found common cause in their perceptions of American power in the world. Roosevelt inherited a country that was disillusioned by the experience of "the war to end all wars" and had persuaded itself that the wisest defense against foreign perils was to ignore them. Eisenhower may well have been the only man of his time who could have successfully guided the United States from its postwar uncertainty to championing a common purpose in the world that transcended party politics. Roosevelt was a stylish aristocrat with a cynical turn of mind; Eisenhower was a plain-spoken officer with the gift of cold judgment. Both were politicians of genius, with a talent for transmuting, in their different ways, private convictions into public inspiration.

A further irony is that Roosevelt, who was nothing if not industrious in his pursuit of American power, and harbored no doubts about the necessity of global leadership, is nowadays remembered not as the enemy of isolation and the commander-in-chief who presided over the greatest military undertaking in American history, but as the architect of the American welfare state. And Eisenhower, who directed the Allied campaign against Nazi Germany, waged the cold war against the Soviet Union, and established beachheads of American power around the globe, is now embraced for his valedictory warning against imprudent defense spending. This is not just to misconstrue what these statesmen said and did, but to misinterpret the meaning of their lives. Both were patriots who consecrated themselves to the service of the United States and guided their country in its methodical embrace of global responsibility. The vagaries of historical memory are such that we cannot know how the legacies of Ike and FDR will play out in the future, or how many times their reputations will rise and fall. But it is certainly important that we see them steady and whole, and understand precisely what they meant, to their time and to ours.

Franklin D. Roosevelt enjoys the distinction of having defeated three historians—Arthur M. Schlesinger, Jr., Frank Freidel and Kenneth S. Davis—in their successive attempts to write a multi-volume biography. Of the three, Frank Freidel's undertaking—*Franklin D. Roosevelt: The Apprenticeship* (Little, Brown, 1952), *The Ordeal* (1954), *The Triumph* (1956), *Launching the New Deal* (1973)—is by far the most satisfactory, although it only takes the story up to January 1934. In 1990 Freidel published *Franklin D. Roosevelt: A Rendezvous With Destiny* (Little, Brown), which remains the best one-volume life of FDR, with the possible exception of *Franklin Delano Roosevelt: Champion of Freedom* by Conrad Black (Public Affairs, 2003). Arthur M. Schlesinger, Jr.'s series *The Age of Roosevelt—The Crisis of the Old Order: 1919–1933* (Houghton Mifflin, 1957), *The Coming of the New Deal: 1933–1935* (1958), and *The Politics of Upheaval: 1935–1936* (1960)—has its admirers, but it suffers from the indiscriminate adulation of most early Roosevelt historiography. The same might be said of the several works on the subject by William E. Leuchtenberg, although his *Franklin D. Roosevelt and the New Deal, 1932–1940* (Harper, 1963) is a useful survey, as is the two-volume study by James MacGregor Burns—*Roosevelt: The Lion and the Fox* (Harcourt, 1963) and *Roosevelt: The Soldier of Freedom* (1970)—which is largely limited to politics and policy. *FDR 1882–1945: A Centenary Remembrance* by Joseph Alsop (Viking, 1982) is a shrewd appraisal by a distant relation.

Bibliography

I am indebted to the nine-volume edition of Roosevelt's presidential papers—*The Public Papers and Addresses of Franklin D. Roosevelt* (1928–1940)—edited by Samuel I. Rosenman and published by Random House in 1941; the three-volume edition of *Franklin D. Roosevelt and Foreign Affairs, 1933–1937* (1969), edited by Edgar B. Nixon and published by the Harvard University Press under the auspices of the Franklin D. Roosevelt Library at Hyde Park; and the three-volume edition of *Churchill & Roosevelt: The Complete Correspondence*, edited by Warren F. Kimball (Princeton, 1984). *Franklin D. Roosevelt and Conservation, 1911–1945* (1957), edited by Edgar B. Nixon and published under the joint auspices of the FDR Library and the National Archives, is of parochial interest, but revealing.

Of studies on the Roosevelt presidency there is no end, but certain volumes could be of special value to the apprentice scholar: *Roosevelt and Howe* by Alfred B. Rollins, Jr. (Knopf, 1962), *Franklin D. Roosevelt as Governor of New York* by Bernard Bellush (Columbia, 1955), *Roosevelt and de Gaulle: Allies in Conflict* by Raoul Aglion (Free Press, 1988), *FDR and the Press* by Graham J. White (Chicago, 1979), *Roosevelt and Hopkins: An Intimate History* by Robert E. Sherwood (Harper, 1948), *FDR and the South* by Frank Freidel (LSU, 1965), and *FDR's Splendid Deception* by Hugh Gregory Gallagher (Dodd, Mead, 1985). Students of Roosevelt's foreign policy might usefully begin with *Roosevelt, from Munich to Pearl Harbor: A Study in the Creation of a Foreign Policy* by Basil Rauch (Creative Age, 1950), which was published in the full tide of postwar iconography, and then graduate to the most authoritative contemporary study, *For the Survival of Democracy: Franklin Roosevelt and the World Crisis of the 1930s* by Alonzo L. Hamby (Free Press, 2004). Memoirs and selections of correspondence from the period include *I Was There* by Fleet Admiral William D. Leahy (Whittlesey House, 1950), *Roosevelt and Daniels: A Friendship in Politics*, edited by Carroll Kilpatrick (North Carolina, 1952), *For the President: Personal and Secret, Correspondence Between Franklin D. Roosevelt and William C. Bullitt*, edited by Orville H. Bullitt (Houghton Mifflin, 1972), *The Roosevelt I Knew* by Frances Perkins (Viking, 1946), *Off the Record With FDR, 1942–1945* by William D. Hassett (Rutgers, 1958), and *Working With Roosevelt* by Samuel I. Rosenman (Harper, 1952).

To the extent that there can ever be an understanding of Roosevelt's "thickly-forested interior," the inquirer might well begin with the four volumes of *FDR: His Personal Letters—Early Years* (Duell, Sloan and Pearce, 1947), *1905–1928* (1948), and *1928–1945*, Vols. I–II (1950)—edited by Elliott Roosevelt under the watchful eye of his mother, and end with *Before the Trumpet: Young Franklin Roosevelt, 1882–1945* (HarperCollins, 1985) and *A First-Class Temperament: The Emergence of Franklin Roosevelt* (1992), both by Geoffrey C. Ward, as well as *Closest Companion: The Unknown Story of the Intimate Friendship Between Franklin Roosevelt and Margaret Suckley*, edited by Geoffrey C. Ward (Houghton Mifflin, 1995).

The literature about Dwight D. Eisenhower is not nearly as voluminous as the Roosevelt library, but it does boast an authoritative, two-volume biography which has not been superseded: *Eisenhower: Soldier, General of the Army, President-Elect 1890–1952* by Stephen E. Ambrose (Simon and Schuster, 1983), and its companion volume, *Eisenhower:*

Bibliography

The President (1984). The student of Eisenhower is also indebted to the 21-volume edition of *The Papers of Dwight David Eisenhower*, which is divided between *The War Years* and *The Presidency*, edited by Alfred D. Chandler, Jr., Louis Galambos, et al. and published by the Johns Hopkins University Press between 1970 and 2001. *Eisenhower and the American Crusades* by Herbert S. Parmet (Macmillan, 1972) is a standard study of Eisenhower's statecraft in peace and war.

Unlike FDR, Ike was a skillful writer, and there are several illuminating volumes by his own hand. Eisenhower's account of his participation in World War II, *Crusade in Europe* (Doubleday, 1948), might well be the best American military memoir since Ulysses S. Grant's. Ike also published two volumes of presidential memoirs under the general title of *The White House Years—Mandate for Change, 1953–1956* (Doubleday, 1963) and *Waging Peace, 1956–1961* (1965)— and his later *At Ease: Stories I Tell My Friends* (Doubleday, 1967) is charming and informative. Two posthumous volumes of diaries have appeared: *The Eisenhower Diaries*, edited by Robert H. Ferrell (Norton, 1981), which concentrates largely on his public career, especially after 1945, and *Eisenhower: The Prewar Diaries and Selected Papers, 1905– 1941*, edited by Daniel D. Holt (Johns Hopkins, 1998). Also of interest is the transcript of a television interview with Alistair Cooke, *General Eisenhower on the Military Church - ill*, edited by James Nelson (Norton, 1970). Three informative accounts of Eisenhower's service in World War II are *Eisenhower as Military Commander* by E. K. G. Sixsmith (Stein and Day, 1972), *Eisenhower: At War 1943–1945* by David Eisenhower (Random House, 1986), and *Eisenhower's*

Bibliography

Lieutenants: The Campaigns of France and Germany 1944–1945 by Russell F. Weigley (Indiana, 1981). John S. D. Eisenhower has published two memoirs, *Strictly Personal* (Doubleday, 1974) and *General Ike: A Personal Reminiscence* (Free Press, 2003).

It is often explained that Eisenhower's reputation among scholars and journalists began to rise with the publication of Murray Kempton's essay, "The Underestimation of Dwight D. Eisenhower" (*Esquire*, September 1967)—"He was the great tortoise upon whose back the world sat for eight years. We laughed at him … and all the while we never knew the cunning beneath the shell"—and in *Nixon Agonistes: The Crisis of the Self-Made Man* (Houghton Mifflin, 1970) Garry Wills pronounced Eisenhower a politician of "genius." But the serious reappraisal of Eisenhower began with the publication of *The Hidden-Hand Presidency: Eisenhower as Leader* by Fred I. Greenstein (Basic Books, 1982) and has continued through a number of studies, including *Waging Peace: How Eisenhower Shaped an Enduring Cold War Strategy* by Robert R. Bowie and Richard H. Immerman (Oxford, 1998), *The Eisenhower Presidency* by Richard V. Damms (Longman, 2002), *Eisenhower and the Cold War* by Robert A. Divine (Oxford, 1981), and *Eisenhower's War of Words: Rhetoric and Leadership* by Martin J. Medhurst (Michigan State, 1994). *The Presidency of Dwight D. Eisenhower* by Chester J. Pach and Elmo Richardson (Revised, University Press of Kansas, 1991) is a comprehensive survey.

Four books of recollections by members of Ike's White House staff would be of interest to the student of the Eisenhower presidency: *No Time for Rest* by Robert Cutler (Little, Brown, 1966), *Eisenhower: The President Nobody Knew* by

Bibliography

Arthur Larson (Scribner's, 1968), *Eisenhower the President: Crucial Days, 1951–1960* by William Bragg Ewald, Jr. (Prentice-Hall, 1981), and *The Ordeal of Power: A Political Memoir of the Eisenhower Years* by Emmett John Hughes (Atheneum, 1963), which may be said to have begun the tradition of self-aggrandizing memoirs by presidential speechwriters. Two interesting volumes that reflect contemporary sentiment among journalists are *Affairs of State: The Eisenhower Years, 1950–1956* by Richard H. Rovere (Farrar, Straus and Cudahy, 1956) and *Eisenhower the President* by Merlo J. Pusey (Macmillan, 1956).

Eisenhower's statecraft is central to two volumes in the series *American Secretaries of State and Their Diplomacy*, namely *John Foster Dulles* (Vol. 17) by Louis L. Gerson (Cooper Square, 1967) and *Christian Herter* (Vol. 18) by G. Bernard Noble (1970), as well as to *Eisenhower and the Suez Crisis of 1956* by Cole C. Kingseed (Louisiana State, 1995). For students of Anglo-American relations in this period, two volumes edited by Peter G. Boyle are essential reading: *The Churchill–Eisenhower Correspondence, 1953–1955* (North Carolina, 1990) and *The Eden–Eisenhower Correspondence, 1955–1957* (North Carolina, 2005), as well as *The Macmillan–Eisenhower Correspondence, 1957–1969*, edited by E. Bruce Geelhoed and Anthony O. Edmunds (Palgrave Macmillan, 2005).

Index

Index

Index